IT'S ALL TRUE

WALKING BY FAITH IN A FUNKY WORLD

Jeff Slaughter
with Randy Winton

Foreword by Amy Grant

Skyhorse Publishing

Skyhorse Publishing books may be purchased in bulk at special discounts for sales promotion, corporate gifts, fund-raising, or educational purposes. Special editions can also be created to specifications. For details, contact the Special Sales Department, Skyhorse Publishing, 307 West 36th Street, 11th Floor, New York, NY 10018 or info@skyhorsepublishing.com.

Skyhorse® and Skyhorse Publishing® are registered trademarks of Skyhorse Publishing, Inc.®, a Delaware corporation.

Visit our website at www.skyhorsepublishing.com.

10 9 8 7 6 5 4 3 2 1

The author is grateful for the use of lyrics from "Testify," copyright 1996, 1998 EMI MUSIC PUBLISHING LTD. and UNIVERSAL/MCA HOLLAND B.V. All Rights for EMI MUSIC PUBLISHING LTD. in the U.S. and Canada controlled and administered by EMI LONGITUDE MUSIC. All rights for UNIVERSAL/MCA HOLLAND B.V. in the Western Hemisphere controlled and administered by UNIVERSAL MUSIC CORP. All rights reserved. International Copyright secured. Used by permission.

Library of Congress Cataloging-in-Publication Data is available on file.

ISBN: 978-1-62087-933-7

Printed in the United States of America

To the Giver of every good and perfect gift . . .
my Friend, my Healer, my Savior . . . Jesus.

To my parents, Carl and Ruth, the two greatest
gifts I could have ever received! Thank you for
teaching me how to laugh, how to love, and how
to stand . . . come what may. What an honor to be
called your son!

—Jeff Slaughter

To God above all, for giving me this opportunity.

To Rachel, my wife, partner, and best friend, and
our sons Caleb, Joshua, Noah, and Jonah . . . all
of whom work together to make my life full.

—Randy Winton

"What is to give light must endure the burning."

—Viktor Frankl

"For He knows the way that I take; and when I have been tested, I will come forth as gold."

—Job 23:10

CONTENTS

FOREWORD

Everybody loves a good story. Add a great delivery to that good story, and without even knowing why, the listener and the story become part of each other. "I had an aunt just like that." "Our family does the same crazy thing!" "I've felt that heart-stopping wave of dread." The truth is, all of us are living out a story; some just happen to be more interesting than others. Maybe it's the way Jeff's rural Mississippi Delta roots push through the cracks in unsuspected ways. . . . Maybe it's the thinness of the veil, between the seen and the unseen world, which he communicates so well. . . . Maybe it's the plainspoken honesty that marks his conversation, with Mama Ruth or with God Himself. . . . Maybe it's because I first heard about his life, which began in Greenwood, Mississippi, at our dinner table, many years ago, when my children were much younger and Jeff was their piano teacher (long before any thought had been given to this book). I love a good story. A good one at the right time can change your life. Reading Jeff's has certainly affected mine."

———Amy Grant

CHAPTER 1

JUMP!

Stephen was like most any other kid I've ever met at a summer camp. First of all, he loved everything about it: the recreation, the Bible study, his group leader, the new friends he was making, and the nightly worship services. And, oh, how he loved to sing! He was adventurous, with this infectious laugh that made his blonde hair bounce.

Every camp has "that kid" to whom every other camper is drawn. Stephen was "that kid." Only a couple of days into camp, he and his dad could barely walk anywhere on campus without hearing someone call out, "Hey, Stephen!" With that bright, toothy grin flashing, he'd wave back and reply, "Hey, hey!"

It's common at camp for me to bring kids up on stage to sing the "Humpty Dumpty" song, do the motions with me for another song, or even to read a scripture. I had hung out with Stephen throughout the week and thought it would be great to honor his passion for life by asking him to read his favorite scripture during one of our worship times. So one night Stephen walked up on stage with his father, opened his Bible, and as his fingers lightly touched the bumps on the page, he read the 23rd Psalm from a Braille Bible to a hushed crowd. Though he was completely blind, Stephen understood that "the Lord is my shepherd; I shall not want." He read with such genuine, sincere, childlike faith, that there wasn't a dry eye in the crowd.

Stephen's dad was a soft-spoken man who adored his son and helped him get around at camp. It was obvious Stephen loved having his dad with him and the conversations and adventures they shared were extraordinary. Because his dad didn't want his son to miss out on anything, it was especially fun to watch them during recreation time. While there would be hundreds of kids running around, Stephen's dad made sure they were right in the thick of things.

Part of the recreation time was spent with kids running down a hill and flinging themselves onto a 40-by-100- foot gray tarp covered in soap and water. Building as much speed as they could, students would try to gain enough momentum to navigate awkward belly flops as gracefully as possible and roll off onto wet, sticky grass on the other side.

Of course, Stephen wanted to be part of the action, and he wanted his dad and me to come along for the ride. I had watched Stephen's father all week long and admired not only how patient and loving he was toward his son, but also how he encouraged him to take advantage of his spirit of adventure. Countless times that week Stephen experienced life at camp just like the rest of the kids.

This day would be no different, and Stephen was beside himself with excitement. The giant slip 'n' slide has always been one of my favorite things at camp, so when Stephen asked me to do it with them, I was ecstatic. His dad explained exactly what we were going to do while Stephen unsuccessfully masked the giggles coming from within him.

"We're all going together. When I say go, you run as fast and as hard as you can straight ahead. When we get close, I'm going to tell you to jump, and when I do, fling yourself out as far as you can onto that slip 'n' slide. Don't be afraid, son. You just jump, and let the soap and the water do the rest. It's gonna be a blast! You ready?"

"Yes, Sir, Daddy, I'm not afraid. I got it!"

"Okay, Stephen. Ready. Set. Go!"

Stephen never hesitated, and he completely left his father and me standing there. He was off like a shot. Neither one of us helped Stephen in any way during that dash, yet he ran straight as an arrow at his target. His face was lit up like a Christmas tree. As we approached, his father was encouraging him to get ready.

Fifteen yards remained, then ten, then five, and his dad yelled, "Jump!"

I WASN'T PLANNING ON BEING WOKEN UP BY MESSAGES BECKONING ME from my phone, but at 6:30 on a cold December morning, that's what happened. I am typically an early riser, but there was one morning following a long week of Thanksgiving travel between Greenwood, Mississippi, where I grew up, and Nashville, Tennessee, where I have made my home for more than twenty-five years, that I wanted to stay under the covers for a little longer.

The first buzz from the phone was no big deal. I stirred a bit, rolled over, and adjusted my comforter around me. I opened one eye, but quickly closed it. A second alert came, then a third and a fourth.

Before I knew it, my phone was vibrating so much that it had nearly shimmied off the nightstand. In a fog of sleepiness, a sudden fear came over me, and I bolted straight up in my bed wondering with sudden clarity if one of my family members in Mississippi was trying to reach me.

When I looked at my phone, there were so many texts, emails, and Facebook messages that I didn't know where to start. It soon became apparent (thank goodness) that none of these messages were beckoning me to come home to some family tragedy.

"Jeff, I just read LifeWay's blog on their website," one message read. "What's going on?" Another said, "Jeff, I just saw the news. So sorry to hear this, but we're praying for the next step in your life." As I scrolled through hundreds of messages on the same subject, one in particular caught my eye. It was from a friend in Oklahoma, and it read, simply, "The end of an era, not the end of a destiny."

As I read through the slew of encouraging messages from friends and strangers alike, I realized what had happened. The announcement of my decision to leave LifeWay had been released to the public. I made my way to my computer, pulled up the LifeWay Christian Resources website, clicked on the VBS blog, and began to read:

For the past sixteen years, millions of children and families through VBS have benefited from a talented and enthusiastic music minister whose name is synonymous with VBS. Jeff Slaughter, the songwriter for LifeWay Christian Resources' Vacation Bible School team, has decided 2012 will be his last season of writing, traveling, performing, and teaching with our VBS team.

God has given Jeff new dreams and new visions. We will miss him and pray that God continues to use him. We want you to join us as we celebrate Jeff and his years of creative ministry at all the upcoming 2012 VBS preview events. At each event, Jeff's contribu-

tions, creativity, and career highlights will be celebrated with a video tribute connected to the performance of the "Amazing Wonders Aviation" musical.

Jeff was originally enlisted in 1997 to create high-energy music written specifically for each year's VBS theme. With the introduction of "The Wild and Wonderful Good News Stampede," Jeff and LifeWay's VBS became synonymous. Since then, Jeff has produced twenty-two VBS themes and 133 songs (including thirty songs specifically for preschoolers) for both the mainline and Club VBS. Jeff's contribution has helped shape VBS as it is known today. His music has reached into the hearts of kids, and the motions he choreographed have helped the lyrics become personal and the message of Christ memorable.

Jeff has also been a highlight of these events, where he shares the stories behind the songs and teaches the accompanying motions first-hand. The VBS team appreciates Jeff and his creative contributions. We've had a tremendous relationship with him. God has not only used Jeff to impact the lives of millions but he has impacted each of us here at LifeWay.

There are pivotal moments in all of our lives when we are defined by how we respond to circumstances. This was one of those moments for me. I wasn't caught off guard by LifeWay's announcement. I had made my decision to leave in November when I realized the Lord was leading us in different directions. Staring at the words on my computer screen, I knew there was no turning back now. The die had been cast, and what had been a terrific sixteen-year run was now over.

Even though I knew I was doing what the Lord wanted me to do, during those early morning hours panic and fear of the unknown began to assault my heart as I wondered about the future. Knowing that my skill set is quite specialized and not something you'd find on Craig's List, I was bombarded with visions of myself standing behind a counter asking, "Would you like fries with that?" However, my phone's constant vibrating reminded me that people all over the world were praying for me, and their words of encouragement brought great comfort.

Like Stephen's story at the beginning of this chapter, I knew I had to place complete trust in my Father. God was asking me to jump into complete darkness and to trust that He knew the incredible joy and revelation awaiting me when I landed.

I am so grateful for the sixteen years I was able to partner in ministry with LifeWay. They gave me an opportunity to build on a dream I had as young boy to lead worship and allowed me to carve out a niche with children's worship music not common in the Nashville music scene.

That niche opened a huge door just a few days later when Brentwood Benson Music called and wanted to develop an entire children's music brand around my name. Brentwood Benson is home to the world's largest Christian music catalog, and its songs have been recorded by virtually every major artist in the Christian music industry, including my dear friend Amy Grant. Even more so, they had established a relationship with Soles4Souls, an organization that was already near and dear to my heart.

In the weeks between my exit from LifeWay and the day Brentwood Benson called, I struggled many times wondering where the Lord was leading me. The Enemy was constantly whispering in my ear that I was finished, that I would lose everything, that my identity was gone. It was difficult not to listen.

But in His gentle, yet powerful way, the Lord kept reminding me that He would honor my trust and faith in Him. I stayed as close as I could to Him and watched in awe as He brought blessings into my life beyond anything I could have ever imagined.

Growing Up Slaughter

BEFORE MY MOTHER PASSED IN 2009, SHE AND I SPENT MANY HOURS going through stories of our family's history. It was important to the both of us that I know everything I could. Little did I realize that *new* information would surface after all these years. Since there are six years between my sister Carla and me, we were talking about why Mama and Daddy had waited so long to have me. As she was recounting the story, I suddenly heard the words ". . . and you were conceived on the living room couch." *What?* I did *not* need to know that.

It seemed on that, uh, fateful night, Mama's parents had come to visit for the weekend. Mama and Daddy owned a small, two-bedroom home, so my two sisters were in one bedroom, and Mama's parents were in the other. My parents were left with the couch. "You know, hon, when you sleep that close together, things happen."

So now, in a nutshell, you have met the Slaughter family. I am a direct product—literally—of a family that loves to laugh and tell stories and is bound with both uncommon love and exceptional strength.

And when I was born in January 1965—one month late and almost eleven pounds—a journey began that has provided stories for laughter as well as ones of profound sadness. Along the way, we have experienced God's grace at a level of pain so deep that we weren't sure He could reach.

Yet we've also felt His peace at a level of joy we never thought we could reach.

Through tragedy and untold sorrow, to immeasurable delight and laughter, I think my Aunt Delores (who we call "Delo") said it best: "Our family laughs so hard together because we have hurt so deeply together."

I am sharing it all in this book.

I grew up in Greenwood, Mississippi, a town of 22,000 that was very Mayberry-like. We loved to play music, go to North Greenwood Baptist Church, and eat Sunday lunch at the Crystal Grill Restaurant. We made our own Halloween costumes and decorated Christmas trees Daddy cut down with popcorn garlands and homemade ornaments. We went swimming in Legion Lake on Sunday afternoons, learned to roller skate at the Twilight Skating Rink, and watched movies at the Twin Cinema on Saturdays. Carla worked there so I got in for twenty-five cents instead of the full price of seventy-five cents and I would stay all day.

I was the youngest of three and the only boy. (My sisters have always called me "Joseph," the favored one from the Bible story.) Vickie was born first, followed by Carla eighteen months later; then the "incident" on the couch produced me some six years after that. My father was a Mississippi Delta man's man and had hoped his son would be as well. However, I loved music from the very beginning, and I can remember straining to reach up high enough to touch the keys on our piano. From the outset, it's all I ever wanted to do, and I came to learn later—despite horrific bullying and self-doubt—that it's what I was born to do.

My parents met and fell in love in 1951 after a game of "Spin the Bottle" at Mama's fourteenth birthday party. Their love affair lasted fifty-two years.

Carl Lee Slaughter was the firstborn son of Fred Alfred and Ora Lee Slaughter. I always thought it was cool that Daddy's birthday was 11/22/33. Three years later his sister, Margie, was born and their family lived in Sumner, Mississippi. He loved woodworking even as a teenager and was an award-winning athlete. His daddy, whom we would have called "Tapaw" had he lived, passed away in 1957 of lung cancer at the age of forty-nine.

Elinor Ruth Pinion was the second of seven children born to Elmer and Louise Pinion in Brazil, Mississippi. Betty Jean was the oldest, followed by Mama then my Uncle Hot, who got his name because of his temper. Four years after, four more babies followed: Aunt Delo, then Aunt Linda, and then Glenn and Mike.

When I was three, Glenn and Mike were killed seven weeks apart in car accidents. Mike was nineteen and a talented musician whose goal was to become a music minister. Of everyone in our family, I am told I'm more like Mike than anybody. He died on November 8, 1968. Glenn, who was twenty-one and had decided to become a minister as well, was killed on December 27, 1968—Mike's birthday.

Faith always played a big part in our family's life . . . and Mama led the way. She fell in love with Jesus at a church service when she was twelve years old—which is not all that unusual in the Bible Belt, until you consider that both her grandfathers and her own daddy were atheists. The first thing she did when she got home was to tell her daddy about the decision she had made. She was so sincere and so sweet when she looked at him with those big, brown eyes and said, "Daddy, I'm going to Heaven, and I just don't want to be there without you." That was all he could take.

Right then and there he called the preacher and told him, "If Ruth feels all this joy, then I want to know more about it myself." By the end of that conversation he told that preacher to "add him to the list" because he was getting baptized with his daughter. I'm told that night when a Pinion—someone from a family whose members were known to mock Christianity—walked the aisle, folks were "jumping the pews" and shouting in praise for what the Lord had done.

And so the foundation was set.

In the following pages, you will read more of my story. There is great joy as well as great sorrow interwoven within these chapters.

I hope what you realize by the end is that God is always there, holding you up and leading you. He has never forsaken the Slaughter/Pinion family, and He will never leave yours either. In whatever way you may connect to my story, I pray that once you have read it, you will not be afraid to stand on that cliff and obey when the Lord says, *Ready. Set. Jump!*

CHAPTER 2

IT'S ALL TRUE

THE GREEN ROOM FLOOR OF THE MOODY BIBLE INSTITUTE IS NOT THE kind of place you want to find yourself curled up in the fetal position, wailing and trembling, but that's where I was and what I was doing a few weeks after my father died in 2003.

Sure, maybe I had a good excuse. After all, the amount of stress from many months of caring for someone terminally ill can't be measured, and the grief that comes with watching someone you love deteriorate so drastically before he finally takes his last breath is more than some can bear. But for me, it went even deeper than that.

It was January 2000, two days after my thirty-fifth birthday, when my sister Vickie called me from Greenwood, Mississippi, with terrible news. Through her tears, she had to tell me that our father, Carl, had Stage 4 spindle cell melanoma, a very aggressive cancer. I was so stunned and so numbed by her words that after I hung up the phone, I couldn't think straight enough to decide what to do next. It felt like the bottom had just fallen out from under me.

My father was only sixty-six years old and lived in Mississippi with my mother, Ruth. My sisters, Vickie and Carla, also lived in Mississippi.

I had been living in Nashville trying to build my music career. After Vickie's call, I began looking around the room simply trying to focus on something. Through my blurred vision and confusion, I saw the awards that hung on my wall and the sheet music sitting on the piano my parents had given me when I was fourteen. And, all of a sudden, I didn't care about any of it any more.

I just wanted to go home.

THE NEW DECADE (AND CENTURY) WAS SUPPOSED TO BRING WITH IT A clean slate. Only sixteen months earlier we had buried my fourteen-year-old niece, Mallorie, after she had been killed in a four-wheeler accident at a Labor Day weekend family reunion. Our emotions were still raw, and we desperately needed a new start.

Having just celebrated my birthday on January 10, it seemed that things were definitely taking a turn for the better. Only forty-eight hours later, though, all that changed with the phone call from my sister.

As I stood looking around my living room, I thought about how in addition to his forty-one-year career as a road construction foreman to support his family, my father had taken the time to become an accomplished carpenter. All of his pieces were beautifully crafted and had some special element that made them uniquely his. In the living room of my duplex sat both a coffee table that was one of his first creations as a high school woodshop student and an entertainment center that he had made for me after he retired. I was teaching piano and voice lessons in the homes of some of Nashville's wealthiest families to help make ends meet. In one particular home was this entertainment center that I loved, but knew I couldn't afford. So I took a picture of it and gave it to my daddy.

From that snapshot, he made an entertainment center that I wouldn't have traded for all of the expensive ones I had seen.

After I looked at the things he had so lovingly made me, I simply did the only thing I knew to do. I picked up the phone and called my friend Amy Fenton, who was the children's pastor at the Church at Brook Hills in Birmingham, Alabama, to ask her to have people start praying for my dad. She emailed the entire staff, and it wasn't long before Rick Ousley, then the senior pastor of Brook Hills, called and said, "Jeff, I just got word about your father from Amy, and I started praying immediately. I felt God tell me to call you and say this: 'Remember, today, it's all true.'"

Over the next few minutes, Pastor Ousley quoted to me, among other scriptures, Psalm 46:1 ("He is a very present help in times of trouble") and 2 Peter 5:7 ("Cast your cares upon Him, because He cares for you"). After every other verse, he would stop and say, "Jeff, remember, today, it's all true."

Because I had performed at children's events at the Church at Brook Hills, Rick remembered some of the lyrics I had sung from VBS songs and worship songs, and he began to quote some of those lyrics back to me. In soothing, hushed tones he would repeat those words I had sung hundreds of times, and every now and then would add, "Jeff, remember, today, it's all true."

My father was everything I wasn't but thought he wanted me to be, so I spent the majority of my life thinking I was a big disappointment to him. He was this rough, tough, hunting, fishing, football-playing, tobacco-chewing, Mississippi Delta man. What he got in me was a tenderhearted musician who liked to fish every now and then. And because he was from that generation of men who rarely expressed affection for their sons, there wasn't much to otherwise sway my idea of our relationship.

When I was younger, I tried to be what I thought he wanted me to be. It seemed as if he didn't think he'd have to teach me anything, that somehow by the miracle of DNA and good genes I would just know things he knew. For example, when I'd go down to his workshop sometimes, I'd feel all anxious because I knew eventually he was going to ask me to retrieve a tool for him. "Son, grab me a Phillips screwdriver." I had no idea what he was talking about, so I'd start sweating and grab the first thing I thought might be the tool, hand it to him, and stand there, hoping against all hope I had somehow—by a miracle of God Himself—handed him the right one. "Phillips!" his big voice boomed when I handed him a flat-head. "I said Phillips! Does that look like a Phillips-head screwdriver?"

One time, when I was nine years old, he thought I might be showing a bit of an interest in bird hunting, so he took me to an Otasco Store on a Saturday morning and bought me a .410 shotgun and three boxes of shells. We went to this old cotton field not far from our home, and close to where my daddy loved to bird hunt.

He actually took a few minutes to teach me how to hold the gun, sight my target, and gently squeeze the trigger when I was ready to shoot. Then he had me shoot a few rounds at a pie-tin target he had nailed to a tree. When he thought I was ready, he took me into the cotton field and left me in a place to hunt all alone. He left his tender-hearted, nine-year-old musician squatting down in a cotton field by himself, with a brand-new weapon that he had shot exactly two times.

To be honest, though, I had a great time. I shot at everything. If it moved, I shot at it. If it was stationary, I shot at it. I used every single shell in those three boxes. And, in the end, three dead birds lay in my wake. Obviously, all the commotion lured my daddy back.

"Daddy, I killed three birds! I killed three birds!" I could barely contain my excitement.

He smiled. "That's good, son. Get your stuff. We're going to go to another spot." Then he looked around. "Where are all your shells?"

"I used them all."

"You shot up three boxes of shells and only killed three birds?"

"Yeah . . . but I killed three birds." I was still pretty proud of my accomplishment. He just turned and walked away.

After that, he had me retrieving his birds. When he clipped one (apparently, he wasn't as good a shot as his nine-year-old son), I saw that the poor bird was still alive, and I ever-so-gently scooped him up and carried him back to my daddy. My heart was breaking for this bird, and I wondered how we might fix him.

"Daddy, he's still alive."

"Yeah."

"Now what?"

He answered that question by grabbing the bird and placing it between the knuckles of his index and middle fingers and swinging it around and around until its head separated from its body. It's called wringing a bird's neck, and I was shocked. After I screamed and all the birds in the surrounding trees flew away, our one and only hunting trip came to an abrupt end.

We just weren't close, my daddy and I. We were so different that there wasn't any part of either of our lives where we related to each other. But I so wanted it to be different. I didn't hunt ever again or fix cars or chew tobacco, but I always wanted to be the best at everything I did, because I desperately wanted to make him proud. When it came to grades, I worked to have the highest grade-point average in the school. It wasn't simply enough to be in a club; I wanted to be elected president. Still, no matter what I did, I never thought it would be enough to measure up.

I was twenty-six when he found it necessary to tell me that if I never married and had sons of my own, our family name would die with me. And that was the last straw. I had been in counseling throughout that year for some abuses I had suffered in my childhood by a family member. It was during that year that my counselor had told me that I needed to write a letter and voice my feelings about my dad. I didn't have to mail it to him, necessarily, but I needed to write it out so that some healing could begin to take place.

Just before his birthday in 1991, I sat down and poured my heart out to him in a letter. In essence, the core of the letter said, among other things:

Daddy: I have hated you all of my life, but now I realize I don't really hate you at all . . . I just don't know you. I don't know your favorite color, what your favorite food is, or what your dreams were as a young man. And you don't know me. If I have problems or issues in my life that require me to seek advice, you are not one of the people I would call. Not only are you not at the bottom of the list; you are NOT ON the list at all. But, in my perfect world this is how you and I would get along . . .

I spelled it all out in the letter, and along with it sent him a recording of a song I wrote for him titled "Never Too Late for Love." I put both in a package to take to the post office, because I knew that if I put it in my own mailbox, I'd probably grab it before the mailman came. A few days later my mom called to tell me he received it on his birthday. "What did he do?" I asked.

"He cried, Jeff. He cried so hard that he shook."

About a month later, I went home for Christmas. I noticed a difference in him immediately. He was more present with us than I'd ever seen before. He would sit down at the table and listen to conversations we were having. At one point I had gone into the guest room to wrap some presents. He walked in, pushed the wrapping paper rolls on the bed out of the way, and sat down. My heart stopped. I couldn't think of anything to say. How do you start a conversation like this? I was so touched, though, because I knew what a huge step this was for him.

"Mama said you got my letter." It took everything in me to get those words out.

"Yeah, I did."

I swallowed hard and fought desperately to hold back my tears. "What did you think about it?"

"It was alright," he said gently.

For my daddy, that said it all. He was a man of few words, but with those three I knew he was telling me that he was ready to start trying to heal the broken places between us. To try and start redeeming all the lost years.

He had finished building my parents' house in the country, and the day after Christmas we started moving their furniture to the new place. We rode in his truck together, and for a while it was pretty quiet, which made it an awkward ride. Finally, he started telling me all these stories about growing up and how he and his dad were so close—"best friends," he said—and when my grandfather died of lung cancer at forty-nine, his world was crushed.

"His nickname for me was 'Buddy,'" Daddy told me. "I couldn't do anything without talking to him first. I was twenty-three, newly married, and had a baby, and he wasn't there to answer my questions anymore. I started getting sick, and the doctor said I was developing ulcers. He told me I had a choice to make. I could either let my daddy's death destroy me, or I could get over it, go home, and be the father and husband I needed to be." And then, in a more somber, near-whisper, he admitted, "I decided that day that if I ever had a son, he would not depend on me the way I depended on my daddy."

"So, you did this on purpose?" I asked incredulously. "Don't you think you went a little overboard?" He just looked at me. Through his embarrassment and my chagrin, somehow we found enough humor in my question that we both were able to laugh.

From that moment on, our relationship blossomed, and for the next eight years we got closer and closer as father and son. Finally, I felt like he was proud of me.

Truth is, he always had been.

ONCE THE INITIAL SHOCK OF MY SISTER'S CALL WORE OFF AND I WAS ABLE to make my way home, I knew Daddy's diagnosis was a death sentence. Because it was Stage 4, the doctor had given him six months to live. In fact, because of the rarity and aggressiveness of this cancer, there were no treatments available.

I remember hearing Daddy say once that if he ever was diagnosed with cancer, he'd just run out in the woods and blow his brains out. As I made the four-and-a-half-hour drive home I couldn't help but think about those haunting words and wondered if he still felt that way. As I drove I began to pray to the Lord, "I've written him a letter, I hunted with him—okay once, but we do go fishing—I wrote him a song, I've tried to do everything I can to build a relationship with him these past few years. Lord, is there anything I haven't done that I need to do?

And I felt the Lord tenderly say, *You've never kissed your daddy.*

When I got to my parents' house, it was late in the evening, and Daddy was already in bed. I went back to see him, and we started talking. My heart began to race when he said, "I always said that if I was ever diagnosed with terminal cancer, I'd go out in the woods and kill myself." I nodded and swallowed hard.

"Well, son. You don't have to worry about that, because God has given me an incredible peace about it. Even though there isn't a treatment. . . ."

"There is a treatment," I interrupted. "We are going to stand on the Word. Tonight I'm going to write down every scripture I can find on healing, and we are going to claim God's healing power over you every day."

As I started to walk out the door to grab my Bible and go to the kitchen table to begin my search of the scriptures, I walked back over to the bed, bent down, and kissed my daddy for the first time in my life. I was thirty-five; he was sixty-six. Instantly, whatever fragments that might still have existed from that emotional barrier that once separated us were completely demolished. He smiled and hugged my neck, and nothing in the world could have meant more to me in that moment.

Over the next several hours I used a Concordance and found every scripture in the Bible on healing; they filled up the front and back of seven pages. When my dad woke up the next morning, I gave him those papers.

"This is your treatment," I said as I handed him the scriptures. "Read these over yourself every single day."

True to his nature, my father was a disciplined man. So, if he said he was going to do something, you could count on him to keep his word, just like one counts on the sun to rise every morning. He read every one of those scriptures every day until the day he died—thirty-nine months later. Those worn and weathered, tear-stained pages that he carried with him everywhere he went sustained him and strengthened him to long outlive the six-month death sentence he was given. At his funeral, his coffin bore a secret drawer, so it was only fitting that those seven pages of scriptures would be placed there.

The Lord truly did redeem the lost years in those three years and three months.

AFTER MY DAD WAS DIAGNOSED IN JANUARY 2000, I STARTED GETTING sick just two months later. My sinuses were flaring, I was always congested, and I could barely sing. I was teaching vocal and piano lessons nearly every day and doing weekend events. I had been working with LifeWay for about three years at that time and had flown out to Glorietta, New Mexico, in April to play for a Ski Explosion event. On the flight over I was so sick that I could barely talk by the time I got there.

I was losing my voice. What I was experiencing was not the normal raspy sound you get from having a "tired voice." Something was wrong, and I was getting really worried. My stress level was already high because through those few months, every time my dad went to the doctor, he got a bad report.

Still, throughout that time, I remember the Lord reminding me, *Jeff, remember, today, it's all true.*

I finally made an appointment with a vocal clinic in Nashville, and the doctor ran a scope down my throat, where it was discovered that a polyp had developed on my vocal cords. The doctor was adamant. "If you don't have surgery to remove it, you will do irreparable damage to your cords, and you will never sing again." I wasn't comfortable with the idea of surgery, so I asked him if there was an alternative. "Why don't we put you on total vocal rest for ten days—no singing or talking for any reason; not a single word—then come back and we'll scope again and see what happens."

Driving home from the clinic, I was wondering what God was doing. First, my daddy was diagnosed with cancer, and now I'd lost my voice. Two of the things I loved the most were being taken from me. When I walked in the house, the first thing I did was to put a message on my answering machine explaining that I would not be returning any calls for a while. Then I contacted some friends and invited them to come over that night and pray with me. My friend, Jenna, brought anointing oil she had gotten on a trip to Israel. We prayed and prayed and spoke of God's faithfulness.

Just before midnight I told the Lord, "With the last words I get to speak for ten days, I will bless Your name. I know I will sing as long as You allow me to. I love You, I trust You, and I know You will be faithful to me." As midnight covered us, those were the last words I uttered for ten days.

With a notepad and pen to write what I needed to say, I did all my voice and piano lessons, my banking, grocery shopping . . . everything by hand. I would mouth the words "I can't talk" to people, and I would write them notes.

On one of those days, I went to a Mapco convenience store down the road, and the lady behind the counter greeted me with a warm smile and a loud, Southern voice. "How ya doin', darlin'?" I mouthed the words: *I can't talk*. She nodded and winked at me like she understood. Yet when I brought the items to the counter to pay for them, she smiled again and then whispered, "Do ya wanna a bag?" Just because I couldn't talk, she whispered to me like that would help us communicate better. I paid for my items and walked out, doing all I could not to laugh out loud.

I have never been in a situation where I felt so handicapped. When you can't talk, you can't go through a drive-thru to order food, pick up a phone and order a pizza or call a friend, or Skype with your family. It certainly makes for awkward—if not comical—situations. I had people talking loudly to me as if I were deaf, and on two occasions I had people grab my notebook after I had written them a note and return written communication to me.

Finally, the ten days passed—albeit very quietly, as I realized I hadn't turned on either the television or the radio throughout that time—and I returned to the vocal clinic to have another scope of my vocal cords.

There was no change.

Again, the doctor insisted I have surgery, then follow with up to a year of vocal rest; and, again, I insisted I didn't have a peace about going through with this procedure. His alternative was to send me to this singing therapy thing where the exercises all consisted of operatic techniques. I eventually voiced my concern to my therapist: "I work with kids and if I sing like this at my events, I won't have any events to worry about cancelling."

All the while, the Lord was nudging me to contact Marjorie Halbert, one of my great music professors at Belmont University and one of my first vocal coaches; she would know what to do to help me. When I called her and explained my situation, her reaction was brief and to the point.

"Get in here."

Within the first thirty minutes of my visit with Marjorie, I knew I wouldn't need to have surgery. With the right vocal and breathing exercises, she had me singing better than I had in months. The interesting thing was that, at the time, I was under contract with Student Life Ministries to record a kids' worship project, and I hadn't been able to lay down the vocals on the tracks. I had written the music but couldn't finish the project because I couldn't sing. This was April, and the camps started in June.

Marjorie led me through the whole process. For the next few weeks, she would coach me through each vocal. She'd warm up my voice, and I'd run straight to the studio and record the songs until we finished the project, right up to the last possible night when I could still meet my deadline.

After my first session with Marjorie, I was scheduled to lead a Disciple Now weekend for more than 500 students at the First Baptist Church in Palmetto, Florida. The schedule had me doing a Thursday night concert, taking Friday off, then leading worship Saturday night and again at their Sunday morning services.

FBC Palmetto is a special place for me. It was one of the first churches to have me lead their VBS week after I began writing the music for LifeWay. We had developed a terrific relationship; they had a thriving children's and youth ministry, and the staff, parents, and all the other people there treated me like one of their own.

Palmetto is one of those beautiful places where you can discover the wonder of God's creation and not be distracted by the "busyness" of life. Yes, people work hard for a living, and there is certainly some of the hustle and bustle of life we all experience, but there is something soothing, serene, and very comfortable about Palmetto.

I was staying with a family from the church whose home overlooked the bay. When I arrived at the church for Thursday's concert, I had already decided on the songs I would sing to lead worship. They were songs that were powerful and worshipful, but wouldn't put a lot of strain on my voice. That meant that there would be no "Humpty Dumpty," a crazy song that I am usually asked to do at every concert I play. While I love doing it because it is so energetic and fun and gives the kids a chance to loosen up before we move to a more serious time, it is particularly hard on my voice. So I didn't even consider it.

Two songs into the event, however, 500 kids started yelling for me to do "Humpty Dumpty," and, try as I might, they would not take no for an answer. This was the third song of the night, and when it was over, my voice was gone.

Panic rose up inside me as I looked at all the students expecting to be led in worship while their leader couldn't sing above a whisper. On my keyboard, I began playing the melody of "I Could Sing of Your Love Forever," a popular worship song at that time, which I knew they would be able to sing without me. As they began to sing, I quit playing and they continued singing a capella. It was truly beautiful, although in that moment I was scared to death.

I walked off the stage, called Marjorie, and whispered, "Help me!"

She told me to go to bed, drink tons of water, and take three or four ibuprofen every four hours throughout the night and the next day. And absolutely no talking. "You don't open your mouth all day tomorrow," she ordered. "Not even a whisper." Since I wasn't supposed to lead anything Friday, it was great timing.

The home where I was staying looked like something out of *The Great Gatsby*. It was this beautiful house that connected to the bay with a walkway to the pier. Just before you stepped out on the walkway, you were covered by the shade of a giant weeping willow tree. On a branch that hung out over the water, the family had mounted a swing. The whole scene was straight out of a Currier and Ives painting.

That Friday was a beautiful April morning with the gentlest of breezes blowing. The serenity of the external environment clashed with the internal panic I was fighting. After all, when your heart has always been focused on leading worship, and it is seemingly taken away, it feels like your life is over. Certainly, the doctor was clear: If I continued singing without surgery, I would destroy my vocal cords. The events of the night before only affirmed what he promised would happen.

Needless to say, I was at a very low point.

I finally gathered myself and allowed the breeze to caress my face until I was able to focus on what the Lord wanted to reveal to me. I lay down on a towel and began reading my Bible when I became aware of a still, small voice beginning to whisper to me. *Jeff, remember today . . . it's all true.*

The breath rushed out of my lungs in a great wave, and, again, through the breeze I could hear Him speak to me. *Remember, today, it's all true.*

Months before, when Rick Ousley had said those words to me over the phone, I thought they would make a great idea for a song, but I never pursued it. But now, there was no doubt God was giving me a song to write.

I had never written a song in silence before. I began envisioning myself playing the chords on the piano, hearing the melodies in my head, and crafting the lyrics the Lord was gently whispering in my ear through that soothing coastal breeze. In just a few hours, the song was completed, and I had experienced a different level of intimacy with the Lord. He had never poured a song into me like that before.

Palmetto is where I found my voice. Not my singing voice, but God's voice, saying to me, *It's okay. I will never leave or forsake you. Remember today and every day—it's all true.*

When I finished writing the song, I wondered if I would ever be able to sing it. With that day of rest, I was able to make it through Saturday night's worship for those students. The next morning, as I began to lead the congregation in worship, I told them what had been happening to me and my family. I briefly told them of my father's prognosis, what had been going on with my voice and the real danger that I may not be able to do this much longer. As I spoke to them, I knew people in the building were praying for me and I felt that "peace that surpasses all understanding" promised in God's Word. It was a sweet, sweet moment.

Two days after I sat on that pier, and only minutes after I went to the choir room to run through this new song—really for the first time—I began to play "It's All True" for a sanctuary full of people.

In a moment, a hush came over the congregation, and you could feel God's presence completely blanketing the hundreds of people sitting in the sanctuary. As I looked around, there were people whose eyes were closed in prayer and worship. Others looked heavenward, while others just soaked in the depth and breadth of the moment.

Something surreal and supernatural was released in me as I sang these words for the first time:

> *It's all true, it's all true*
> *Everything Your Word says about You*
> *Every chapter, every verse*
> *Every promise I've ever heard*
> *It's all true, it's all true*

And I want my life to be living proof
That no matter what I go through
It's all true

You are my Shepherd, You are my Savior
You are my Friend, You are my Healer
You are my Refuge, You are my Mercy
You are the Grace sufficient for my needs

It's all true, it's all true
Everything Your Word says about You
Every chapter, every verse
Every promise I've ever heard
It's all true, it's all true
And I want my life to be living proof
That no matter what I go through
It's all true

You never leave me, I am safe in Your hands
You love me more than I can comprehend
You give me comfort to cover my sorrows
You give me hope to face tomorrow

It's all true, It's all true
Everything Your Word says about You
Every chapter, every verse
Every promise I've ever heard
It's all true, It's all true

And I want my life to be living proof
That no matter what I go through (You are)

Wonderful, Counselor
Mighty God, Prince of Peace
You wipe away every tear from my eye
And I can do all things through You, Lord
Who gives me strength
I count it all joy because I believe

It's all true, it's all true
Everything Your Word says about You
Every chapter, every verse
Every promise I've ever heard
It's all true, it's all true
And I want my life to be living proof
That no matter what I go through
It's all true

ON WEDNESDAY, MARCH 19, 2003, MY FAMILY KNEW THAT OUR FATHER was about to leave this life. I was in the shower that morning begging God for a miracle that would not come. I wanted that miracle so badly that I felt if my dad's cancer wasn't healed, I wasn't sure I could ever sing that song again.

Through my bitterness and tears, it was as if the Lord paralyzed me. *Your daddy is the one laying in that bed, not you. Yet he has never once blamed Me, or questioned Me, or cursed Me, or even asked Me why he's had to go through this. He has only praised Me, thanked Me, blessed Me, and been a testimony of My faithfulness to everyone who has come to see him. If he can do it, in the middle of all his pain and suffering, you can do it.*

My father had been in hospice care for six months and Lorrine, his nurse, normally had Wednesdays off. However, she showed up that morning at about 11:00, before I got in the shower, and walked into my father's room, which was full of family and friends. We were shocked to see her. My Aunt Margie said, "Lorrine, you're supposed to be off today." She responded, "Well, I feel like Mr. Carl has a very special appointment today, and I want to make sure he looks just right. He's very modest about himself, so everyone needs to leave the room 'cept me and Mr. Jeff."

Once everyone left the room, she gave him a sponge bath and said, "Jeff, get your daddy some real underwear out, and some khaki pants and a nice shirt." As I helped, it was bittersweet, and the weight of his impending death was heavy on me. Gently, Lorrine finished combing my daddy's hair, bent down to kiss his cheek, and said, "I love you, Bubbles. I'll see you real soon." She had called him Bubbles from the very first day she met him, and I never knew why. She rose up and looked at me. "You know why I call yo' daddy 'Bubbles?'"

"No," I said. "But I've always wondered."

"'Cause from the very first time I came in this room, he made me bubble inside. So I call him 'Bubbles.'"

She left at about 11:45, and I went to take my shower. After I had the encounter with the Lord while in the shower, I heard a knock at the bathroom door; it was Jim Pilgreen, a dear family friend and one of my daddy's best buddies. "Jeff, your daddy's going. You need to get in here." I threw a towel around me and ran into his room and jumped on the foot of my parent's bed, which sat next to the hospital bed where my daddy was lying.

His breaths were weak and labored, and it was obvious he was fighting death. Most of our family had within the last few days told Daddy it was okay for him to go. My mother never had. Watching him struggle so, this look of resolution came over her face for the first time.

At that moment, she knew he needed to hear from her that it was okay for him to let go. She bent over and pressed her face as close to his as she could get. "I've loved you since I was fourteen years old. I remember the first time I saw you come into my mamma and daddy's house. I thought you were the best looking thing I'd ever seen. And you still are. But I want you to rest. You have fought really hard, and I am so proud of you. I'm gonna be okay. I don't know how I'm going to make it without you, but the Lord will help me. There is no time in Heaven, so when you get there, you'll turn around, and I'll be there. I'll feel like I have to wait, but you won't."

A slight grin came over his face, and with his final ounce of strength, he puckered up his lips, and she kissed him for the last time. Once she rose back up, he released his last breath and died peacefully at 12:03. They had fifty-two years together, forty-eight as a married couple, and in that moment I remember feeling so proud to have been blessed with parents who had a legacy of such an enduring love.

My mama was as fine a Southern lady as one would ever meet. True to her nature, she informed me that my daddy needed to be buried in a new shirt from JC Penney to go with his favorite tie, which I bought for him when I was in Italy. Since my parents lived in the country, cell phone service was not great. Once I arrived at JC Penney, my phone began to load all these messages I had received the previous day. I decided to check them before going into the store, so I sat down on the sidewalk and pressed "play."

The first one had come in at 11:50, the exact time when I had gotten in the shower that previous morning, just minutes before my daddy took his last breath: "Hey, Jeff, this is Josh. The Lord is telling me to pray for you right now, and it's so strong. I don't know why, but I'm praying." Then, at 11:52: "Hey, Jeff, this is Rob. I had this strong feeling that God wanted me to pray for you, and I felt like I needed to call and let you know." At 11:53, Naomi called: "Hey, Jeff, I don't know what's going on, but God is telling me to share Psalm 56 with you. 'When I am afraid, I put my trust in you. In God, whose Word I praise, in God I trust and am not afraid. What can mere mortals do to me? . . . You have collected all my tears in your bottle. . . . This I know, God is on my side.'"

All the while I had been battling my anger with God, He was quickening my friends to call me. Standing in that shower just moments before my daddy was to meet the Lord he never questioned, I had challenged the Lord myself. "Here's the deal. I have traveled all over the world telling people to trust You, to love You, and that they can move mountains with their faith. I've been praying with every ounce of faith I've got in me, and You haven't moved the mountain for me today." The mountain for me in that moment was the fact that Daddy was strangling to death. In my heart I kept begging the Lord to just take him instead of letting him linger like that. "I've never prayed for anything harder in my life than for my daddy to live, but I can let him go. I just can't watch him strangle to death," I continued. "If he does, my heart will never be the same. I will never be able to sing 'It's All True' again or lead worship again, because I'm not sure if I can believe it all anymore."

The Lord paralyzed me in a Job-type moment, almost like He was saying, "Who do you think you are, and where were you when I created the universe?" and went on to remind me of how my daddy had handled his illness.

Sitting on that sidewalk, I counted seven messages on my phone. It wasn't lost on me that the number seven in the Bible represents completion. In the midst of my pain, God was teaching me that His plan for my daddy here on earth was complete.

But even though I trusted Him, I was still struggling. Despite that struggle over the next couple of weeks—or maybe because of it—God provided an opportunity for me to get away and sing backup with my dear friend Kim Hill at a conference at Moody Bible Institute in Chicago, where world-renowned Christian author and speaker Jill Briscoe would be sharing a message.

To be brutally honest, even though I was at this event, singing backup with an amazing artist like Kim Hill, and even though there were hundreds of people worshipping with us, I looked around with weary, distant eyes, wondering if I really believed all this anymore.

When it came time for Jill to speak, I sat down and listened as she began to share from Psalm 137, where the children of Israel, held in captivity in Babylon, had "lost their song" and had hung their harps up in the branches of the willow trees because their weeping and bitterness made them not want to sing anymore.

"Have you lost your song today?" Jill asked the large crowd. "Have you hung your harp in a tree? Maybe a tree of grief?"

I knew I was in trouble then. There may have been hundreds of people there, but God was using her words to speak to me.

She went on to tell the moving story of her best friend, whom she had known throughout her childhood, and who was dying of cancer.

Soon, her friend would leave her young daughter behind. She knew dying meant missing out on the biggest events of her daughter's life: first dates, proms, graduations, weddings, and being a grandmother. "So she asked me to be there for all those moments," Jill explained. "I told her she could count on me, and that it would be a privilege to be there for her."

And over the years Jill honored that commitment and shared those special moments with her "daughter." She grew up to be a fine woman, was married, and started a family of her own. Tragically, she was diagnosed with the very same cancer that took her mother's life years before. Her husband called Jill to come when they realized the daughter's time was near. When Jill made it to her bedside, she was so sick and weak she could barely speak. It was obvious, though, that she was trying desperately to tell Jill something, and working very hard to get those last important words out.

As Jill told the hushed crowd, "I got as close to her as I possibly could. I told her if she could just whisper to me what she was trying to say, I would be her voice to the world."

The woman finally mustered the strength to barely whisper the words she wanted her dear Aunt Jill to hear and to share. "Jill, you have to tell everybody . . . it's . . . all . . . true."

When I heard those words, I could not contain my emotions any longer. I jumped from my seat and ran to the Green Room, and I cried and cried and cried. For a long time I lay in the fetal position in the middle of the carpeted floor and wailed as my body shook.

As I look back at all that connected me to that moment, it was obvious that the Lord put me in a place to hear that message. He spoke to me blatantly, strategically . . . intimately.

And, at that moment, I knew I would sing that song for the rest of my life.

CHAPTER 3

CHICKEN AND KETCHUP

By THE TIME I HAD LIVED THROUGH THE NIGHTMARE OF MIDDLE school and had finished my freshman year of high school, I was determined at all costs to be popular by the end of my sophomore year. So I began to work out like crazy, play a lot of tennis, and didn't so much as look at a glass of sweet tea for two years. Even on the hottest of days, when my Mama's gallon of home brew—two cups of sugar notwithstanding—beckoned me from the refrigerator, I did not succumb to this ice cold temptress. As a result, I became a new man.

Even to me, my transformation was amazing. By the beginning of my junior year, I had dropped from a forty-two-inch waist to a thirty-two and rid myself of my glasses (Nanny, Daddy's mother, bought me my first pair of contact lenses). The change was so drastic that some of the students at my large high school were asking if I had just transferred there.

During the last two years of high school, I achieved nearly every goal I had set for myself. I had gained a certain amount of popularity, had won several academic awards, and was very involved in school activities. While at one point I set out to impress my daddy with high grades and lofty positions in clubs and school organizations, I was finally pretty pleased with the person I had become.

A discovery I made while attending a Pat Benatar concert at Mississippi State in Starkville really stoked my desire to attend MSU: Fraternity Row. Until that night, I had bounced around the idea of applying to a few schools. Daddy wanted me at Mississippi Delta Community College in nearby Moorehead, but I wasn't interested in MDCC for two reasons. First, it was a two-year school, and, second, there wasn't anything I wanted to major in there. I really just wanted to get away from Greenwood and start somewhere else. By my senior year, I was pretty determined that the somewhere else was Mississippi State University.

That wasn't even a consideration, as far as my daddy was concerned. He liked to have his family close, and the thought of me moving so "far away"—Starkville was less than an hour-and-a-half away—did not set well with him. In fact, when my sister Vickie left for Delta State University, which was only forty-five minutes away, he laid across his bed all day and cried.

Even so, I was adamant. "Daddy, I don't want to go to Moorehead. I want to go to Mississippi State."

And this is when he drew a line in the sand. "Well, boy, if that's where you want to go, then you can pay for it yourself."

Fine.

Fortunately, one of my favorite teachers, Miss Kay Hankins, told me about a scholarship opportunity through the Shell Oil Company. The Century Three Leaders Scholarship was a nationwide program that sought intelligent young minds that could be molded through higher education to find solutions to twenty-first-century global issues. Through school and state competitions, the selection committee annually picked 102 students nationally to come together in Williamsburg, Virginia, at a conference to debate some of those issues, including education reform, endangered species, children at risk, America's economy, and the environment, as well as American foreign policy in a changing world. But first, each state and the District of Columbia would choose ten finalists from which two winners would be sent to Virginia for the national competition.

Miss Hankins was one of my biggest cheerleaders. A few months earlier, she had encouraged me to compete in a speech competition in Jackson by doing a dramatic interpretation of "No Snakes in This Grass," a one-act play written by James Magnuson. Normally the play has three characters (God, Adam, and an ethnic Eve), but for this competition I was to consolidate the performance down to one character and tell the story. Miss Hankins wrote an opening paragraph for me to memorize as part of the introduction to what I would perform. I remember looking at the first sentence and feeling the panic rise within me. Even though I had spent a lot of time around Miss Hankins, I had been able to hide from her the pronounced lisp I'd been fighting since the fourth grade.

I swallowed hard and read aloud, "On the sthurfasth, 'No Sthnakesth in thisth Grasth' appearsth to be a humoruth thatire at the sthtory of creasthion."

Before that moment, even though I had been in the junior play and was to be the lead for the upcoming senior play, Miss Hankins hadn't realized that I had such a speech impediment (I had learned to hide it by saying as few "s" sounds as possible). I watched her expression slowly change from pleasant anticipation to confusion, to shock, then to amazement before culminating in a wide-eyed "uh oh."

"Umm, Jeff? You have a lisp of some kind that I've never noticed before," she said as gently as she could. Instantly, though, her mission was to help me, because she knew I was mortified. "I can't believe I'm just noticing this after two years, but don't worry. We can fix it. I have a friend named Cathy Cook who will work through every line of this with you. If anybody can help you clear this up, Cathy can."

Miss Hankins was right, because Cathy Cook was amazing. She knew how to make me understand what to do with my tongue and was incredibly patient with me. She came once a week and we went through every single "s" word in my speech. We worked right up until the day before I travelled to Jackson for that speech competition, and with new confidence and no lisp, I won my division title.

So, with determination in my heart and MSU's Fraternity Row in my sights, I wrote what I was sure was the winning essay for the Century Three Leaders Scholarship committee. I entered into this competition with the attitude that it was mine, no matter what. Part of my resolve came from the determination to show my daddy I could do it, and the other part was that I simply wanted the scholarship. I was going to succeed or die trying. I knew I'd gain the nomination from my school, and I was pretty confident I could win the state nomination as well, which could all lead to scholarship money for my first year of college. If I was selected as one of the ten finalists, there would be an interview following a luncheon in Jackson at the state capital. Miss Hankins told me she would coach me on how to conduct myself with proper etiquette and how to answer questions during the interview.

Not long after, Mrs. Beverly Smith, who was a vocational technology teacher and the sponsor of the school's chapter for Future Business Leaders of America (FBLA), approached me about applying for a FBLA scholarship. While I knew what FBLA was—my sister Carla had been involved with it—I didn't have any other connection to it. I'll be really honest; I didn't know the first thing about business, and I sure wasn't up on most of the critical issues facing America. But I did know that the Lord seemed to be making opportunities for me in areas where I didn't really feel I was gifted.

In order to go before the state committee and take the test, I first had to join FBLA a week before the competition. On the day of the test, I remember flipping through the study manual like a fiend. It was the first time I'd even looked at the material, and I pretty much guessed at every question on the multiple-choice test, using a kind of "ABBACADAB-BA" method to choose my answers. For the interview I basically thought about what my Greenwood Country Club band members had taught me a few years before: If you don't know it, fake it 'til you make it.

At the end of the day, the FBLA committee posted the names of all the winners of each category. As I made my way to see how many of my classmates had been successful in their respective interviews, there was a buzz in the air about something. When I got to the board where all the names were posted, to my amazement, I had been chosen as Mississippi's Mr. FBLA. *How did this happen?* I wondered. I mean, a week ago I wasn't even a member, and two hours ago I was cramming as much information as I could on the ride over. And now, I'm about to go on stage and accept this award in front of people who eat, sleep, and breathe FBLA. I felt like such an imposter . . . but not so much that I would turn down the scholarship.

Soon after that, an envelope came to my house bearing the Shell Oil Company logo. I opened it and found what I had hoped, that I had, indeed, been named one of the ten semifinalists and was invited to the luncheon at the capital in Jackson to interview with the state school board for the final portion of the competition.

On the day of the luncheon, Mama woke me up at 6:00 a.m. to have breakfast and get my clothes ironed before I left. "Mama," I said, while I was generously pouring ketchup over eggs and bacon, "everybody wears their clothes wrinkled now. That's the style," I pleaded my case.

"Well, your name ain't 'everybody,' and you are not wearing wrinkled clothes to that interview. If you want to look like a slob, go right ahead, but if anyone would have ever told me that a son of mine would want to wear wrinkled clothes to an interview with the state of Mississippi's school board with a chance of winning a scholarship that would cover his whole college education, I would never have believed it."

And so it began. Throughout the years, my sisters and I knew all too well that once Mama started in with one of her "If anyone would have ever told me" tirades, the best thing we could do was keep our mouths shut and just let her roll.

So, after I had ironed my pants and shirt, delinted my blue blazer, shined my penny loafers, and straightened my sock tie just right, the "mama questions" really started.

"Do you have directions?" she asked.

"Yes."

"What time do you have to be there?"

"Nine."

"Did you put gas in the car? You know you're bad about running out of gas. And what about the tires? Did you check the air in your tires?"

"Yes, Mama." I lied. I would put gas in the car on the way, and probably kick a tire or two to make sure they weren't low.

"So, what are y'all doing for lunch?"

"Not sure. I think the interviews will take most of the day, so they are having lunch in a room there at the capitol."

"So, it's a sit-down, formal luncheon?"

"I guess so."

"Well," she sat straight up and gave me the look. "Let me tell you something, son. I'd almost bet that at a luncheon like this with a lot of people, they are going to serve fried chicken. If they serve fried chicken, and you put ketchup on it, don't you even think about coming back to this house. Mark my word, I will beat yo' tail black and blue! If you put ketchup on your chicken, they're going to think you're a redneck, and you are going to lose that scholarship."

"Yes, ma'am."

Something inside me knew she was right. She realized that this was my opportunity to get where I wanted to be, and she was determined that a bottle of ketchup was not going to stand in the way.

Sure enough, when I walked into the banquet room and saw the long row of chafing dishes, I noticed that the first one was full of fried chicken. To my horror, on every table was a bottle of ketchup. As I looked longingly from one to the other, I heard my mama's words ring in my ears: "Mark my word . . ." As much as I wanted to put the two together in a marriage of dining delight, I knew I'd better not cross my mama. So, I choked that dry chicken down and smiled the whole time at the state board of education members who would interview me after lunch.

A few weeks later, I was summoned over the school intercom to come to the principal's office. I knew exactly what it was all about. When I entered Mr. McHann's office, he was smiling broadly and said, "The state school board just called . . . and you won!" I think he was as proud as I was for this accomplishment.

Walking back to class, I remember feeling that the Lord was letting me know: *Trust Me. Follow Me. I know the plans I have for you.*

I couldn't wait to drive over to the County Market grocery store where Mama worked to tell her what had happened. "I told you," she said with tremendous satisfaction. She was ecstatic. "If you'd have sat there dipping your chicken in ketchup all day, you'd have never had a chance."

Mama always loved to tell a good story, so I'm sure everyone who came through her line the rest of that day heard how I was able to eat my chicken without ketchup—and win a scholarship in the meantime.

CHAPTER 4

THANKS IN EVERYTHING

W HEN I ARRIVED AT MISSISSIPPI STATE UNIVERSITY WITH VISIONS OF Fraternity Row dancing in my head, the thought never crossed my mind that once I figured out I had no clue what degree program I was going to pursue, my days were numbered. Maybe I should have chosen a college based on what best fit my higher ambitions rather than what fraternity I might pledge.

Even though I wanted to study music, I shied away because everyone was in my ear telling me I'd never be able to make a living from it. I attended a mandatory orientation before the fall semester and was told we had to "choose a major" then and there. I had been thinking, *I can debate pretty good. Maybe I should try pre-law.* But when a few of my friends said they were going to study mechanical engineering, I decided to go for that. I found out real quick that to get into the mechanical engineering program, I had to take a placement test. My results came back accompanied by a letter that basically suggested I "reconsider my major" and look for another focus of study.

When school started in the fall, Don Lancaster, my first friend at State and fraternity brother, who lived in the dorm room next to mine, told me he was going to be an accounting major. That sounded good to me, so that's what I signed up for next. The first semester blew by pretty quickly, and most of my classes were core/prerequisite stuff, so I handled them fairly well. Besides, I had been a straight-A student in high school. Now I was able to focus on the real reason I chose Mississippi State: to pledge a fraternity.

If you think my daddy didn't want me to go to MSU because he considered it a "big-shot school," you can only imagine what he thought of fraternities. "Fraternities are for big shots, too. All you're gonna be doing is drinkin' all the time, failing your classes, and gettin' kicked out of school." He made his point pretty clear, which is why one of the first things I did once I arrived on campus was to promptly pledge Kappa Alpha. By the end of my first week of school I was selected as pledge class president.

I had to figure out a way to pay my pledge dues without my parents finding out. So I utilized two sources. One was playing dinner music at the Starkville Country Club on weekends. The other was a little more complicated, and unwittingly involved my mama. Daddy wanted me to make it on my own, and discouraged Mama from sending me any money. But she'd sneak four twenty-five dollar checks to me every month. This was called my "spendin' money." Between this and the money from the country club, I had enough to pay my fraternity dues.

Late in the fall, Kappa Alpha sent a letter congratulating those parents whose sons were pledged into the fraternity. What happened next was not a phone call I wanted to experience. Mama called me at the dorm and gave me a tongue lashing I will never forget. Of course it started with, "If anybody would have ever told me that a son of mine would lie to me . . ." and the rest was a blur. She was wearing me out, but as the youngest and the only boy in the family, I had learned how to work her, and I was pretty good at turning a situation around on a dime whenever she was upset with me. So, by the time she had gotten everything off of her chest and took a breather, I said as innocently as I could, "But, Mama, they elected me pledge class president."

She gasped. "Really? Oh my goodness, I'm so proud of you. I've got to go, hon. I've gotta call Ann Ricks and tell her all about it." Mrs. Ricks was one of Mama's best friends, and Mama told her everything. I was quite pleased that even though I no longer lived at home, my diplomacy skills were still as sharp as ever.

When the second semester started, I took a business calculus class—finite math—and after the second session I said, "I'm out." During the class, the professor had administered a test, which I promptly failed. Badly. I looked over at Don and told him, "I'm done." I walked out and made a beeline straight to my advisor. When I told him that I needed to drop my math class, he growled, "You're an accounting major. You can't drop your math class! It's required for accounting majors!"

"Well, I don't like it."

"Son, if you don't like this class, you've got a looooong road to go."

"You know, I think I want to major in music." I said it as if I were talking to a long lost friend.

"Why do you even want to go to college then?"

"To become a better musician and sharpen my skills."

"Well, then you need to go somewhere else."

While I was firmly entrenched in Kappa Alpha, I was also involved in the Baptist Student Union and played in the BSU band. While at first my focus was on KA, it wasn't long before the Lord was using my friends in BSU to keep me from wandering too far. "The Fishermen" was the name of our band, and the memories of the times we shared together remain some of the fondest I've had in my life. One of my buddies in the band was a guy named Peyton Rawls. I shared with him my desire to study music and to find just the right place to go. He told me about Belmont College (which eventually became Belmont University a few years later) in Nashville, a liberal arts college which boasted a nationally recognized school of music. I had never heard of Belmont, but I started looking into it. I asked The Fishermen to continually pray with me for God's direction, and I knew that if He wanted me to go to Belmont, He would make a way for it to happen.

A year later, in March 1985, I went to Belmont and auditioned to see if I could get into the School of Music. If I got in, I figured I could work and save money to pay for school. I was accepted after that audition, and God provided for me in every way over the next three years.

That summer, my dad got a promotion at work, which meant a pay raise. At the time, I was still driving the "Pinto Bean," the brown 1975 Pinto I had been using for four years. It had been passed down from my sister Carla, who drove it in high school some ten years before. With Daddy's raise, Mama talked him into buying me a more reliable car, because I would be driving five hours to Nashville. So, they spent $6,000 for a brand-new, baby blue Plymouth Horizon.

I wanted to move to Nashville as soon as possible and get acclimated to my new surroundings and spend the summer working and saving money. David Smith, who was part of The Fishermen, was from Franklin, and he told me about his grandmother, Minerva Alexander, who took in boarders. I moved into her home over Memorial Day weekend.

Everyone should have a Minerva Alexander in his life—a person with just enough wisdom to teach you how to live and just enough zest to make you appreciate the joy of living. Minerva squeezed every ounce out of every day, and for the three years I was around her, she proceeded to instill in me a passion for life that I would carry with me forever.

Even at age seventy-three, she was more like a 1960s flower child than she was a senior citizen because she was spunky and "cause" oriented. If she felt she could make a difference somehow, she would jump in with both feet. The first summer I was with her, she took me and two of her teenage grandsons, Mark and Jamie, to "Dying for a Drink" seminars at the Millview Community Club. These classes were designed to teach people how to recognize family members with drinking problems. Her grandsons and I were miserable every minute we were there, and by the time these sessions were over, we were all dying for a drink ourselves.

I loved everything about her, because everything about her was genuine. In her kitchen was a small, round table where we ate dinner. Mimi, as her grandchildren referred to her, made the best dinner rolls and frozen chocolate ice cream cake on the planet. But she really loved to make coleslaw—the vinegary kind—for every single meal. After dinner, we'd sit around that little table and talk for hours. She was a great talker, but an even better listener. I talked to her about everything there was to talk about when it came to my life. When the ugly abuse from my past seemed to catch up with me and threatened to ruin my life again, she patiently and quietly listened to my story and loved on me for an entire weekend until I could manage to meet with a counselor.

To be sure, there were a lot of things about Minerva Alexander that were special. But the greatest character trait she possessed was her faithful walk with the Lord. She had long ago memorized Psalm 139 and could say every word at the drop of a hat. She'd go to church, where people would ask her to quote that passage, and without hesitation she'd recite it verbatim. It was an impressive feat.

Throughout my first year at Belmont, Minerva never charged me a dime to live at her house, not even for groceries. So I would mow the grass and help her keep her beautiful home clean and go to the grocery store with her. I guess she thought if any college student would stay home on a Saturday night and watch *The Golden Girls* with her, they might as well be family. To this day, I will watch *The Golden Girls* because of her, and I can still hear her contagious laughter.

"A grateful heart never has a reason to complain," was something Minerva said often. The first time I heard her say that, I thought, *I'm gonna try to live by that saying myself.* Years later I wrote a VBS song titled "Thanks in Everything" and used Minerva's words of wisdom in the chorus: "A grateful heart never has a reason to complain, so I will thank You in my joy; I'll thank You in my pain."

Minerva died in 1999, and I was asked to lead worship at her service. It was such a privilege. At the end, her grandson, Mark Smith, walked to the pulpit, smiled, and put the perfect cap on the service to honor the legacy of his beloved grandmother.

He quoted the 139th Psalm.

CHAPTER 5

BIRTH OF THE BELMONT RECEPTION

I'VE ALWAYS BEEN SO PROUD TO SAY THAT I'M A DELTA BOY.

The Mississippi Delta is rich in tradition, with unique racial, cultural, and economic history in a landscape that sprawls between the Mississippi and Yazoo Rivers in the northwest section of the state. It is both beautiful and prone to devastating floods. Yet it is like no place on earth. *Southern Living* magazine once referred to the Delta as "a back-road traveler's paradise."

It is a place with deeply entrenched roots in Delta blues, jazz, and rock and roll music—all born out of the poverty of African American sharecroppers and tenant farmers. Music and agriculture have long been the mainstays of the Delta economy. Author David L. Cohn famously described the location of the Mississippi Delta as "beginning in the lobby of the Peabody Hotel in Memphis and ending on Catfish Row in Vicksburg."

Over the years, it has become a region of the state with such diversification that remnants of its agrarian heritage are scattered all along the lower Delta. Larger communities along the way have fostered economic development in education, government, and medicine, while the farming of everything from corn, soybean, rice, and cotton to catfish and poultry has assumed greater importance than ever before. Having grown up around my grandaddy and Uncle Hot farming like they did, I still get a lump of sweet nostalgia in my throat at the smell of pesticides.

Because of the diversity, music, and traditions of the Delta, places like Greenwood, Yazoo City, Batesville, Belzoni, Leland, and the like celebrate their deep roots with days-long events such as the Delta Jubilee, Highway 61 Blues Festival, Mississippi Delta Blues and Heritage Festival, Riverfest, World Crawfish Festival, and, of course, the Juke Joint Festival.

To be sure, there is a certain amount of pride in celebrating such a rich tradition that is known the world over. On a hot August day, there's nothing better than sitting under the shade of a big pecan tree, sipping a glass of iced tea, and listening to the sounds of "Old Man River" behind the levee. One can understand why the Mississippi Delta is considered to be "The Most Southern Place on Earth."

FROM FIRST GRADE ON, I WAS TAUGHT ABOUT GREENWOOD LEFLORE, the principal Chief of the Choctaw Indians long before Europeans migrated to America. But as the numbers of the new Europeans settling in the area increased, both the Choctaw and Chickasaw Indian nations found themselves more and more encroached upon. By 1830, Chief LeFlore and other leaders ceded most of their land to the United States in exchange for land in what is now Southeastern Oklahoma.

Maybe because the chief didn't cause much trouble, the government and the state of Mississippi honored him by naming the town where I grew up Greenwood—in Leflore County, no less.

Some seventy years later, Greenwood would become home to a mile-long stretch of road called Grand Boulevard, which would eventually become regarded throughout the country as "America's Most Beautiful Street." That's because Sally Humphries Gwin, a charter member of the Greenwood Garden (pronounced "Gaaad'n") Club, decided in 1916 to have 1,000 oak trees planted to line up on both sides of Grand Boulevard.

Needless to say, pride in the town of Greenwood runs deeper than the roots of the nearly one-hundred-year-old trees that line the boulevard. "The Gem City of the Delta," Greenwood's own tradition of music and Southern hospitality goes back way before the days when B. B. King first broadcast his live show from WKRM on Howard Street in 1940.

Steeped in such tradition, Greenwood, like most of the Delta region, thrives on its reputation for music, food, and fun, and rightly takes its place among some of the South's best-kept secrets as a place for families to enjoy the good life without having to be wealthy to do so.

Just try on for size the "Que on the Yazoo" barbecue competition that kicks off the annual River to the Rails Festival every May, which coincides with the opening of the Downtown Greenwood Farmers' Market and the Howard Street Pet Parade. With lots of music provided by bands such as The Krackerjacks (the "Party Band of the South"), Blue Mountain, Memphis-based The Plantation All-Stars, and Greenwood's own Howard Street Band, which features a local attorney and a farmer, the River to the Rails Festival draws thousands every year.

Greenwood is deeply Southern, and deeply traditional, which is why it is such a great place to grow up. It's also why Greenwood provided the perfect backdrop for the film adaptation of *The Help*, the wildly popular novel by Kathryn Stockett.

I tell you all of this because you need to know some background of my home to understand why my mama and her buddy Ann Ricks insisted on bringing a little bit of Greenwood charm to Nashville my senior year at Belmont University . . . and why I thought I would be mortified when she told me what she planned to do.

You also need to know that in Mississippi, every life event has to be accompanied by a "reception." I'm not lying. *Every* life event, including anything from recitals to exploratory surgery. True story: When my mom went into the hospital for a procedure to explore the depth of her pancreatic cancer, she had—ahead of time—fixed up a basketful of food, drinks, silverware, napkins, and so forth for us to enjoy in the waiting room.

For every piano recital I had growing up, we could bet on an elaborately decorated reception, the kind that featured one of my mom's yearly staples, which were small, white-frosted petit fours, topped with green icing delicately scrolled in the form of treble and bass clefs.

So it really should not have come as a surprise years later when, as I was preparing for my senior recital at Belmont, my mama started planning a reception for me.

"Well, hon, what do you want to have for your reception?" she asked me one day over the phone.

I panicked. "Mama, people around here don't do receptions."

"Well, you're having one, so you might as well tell me what you want."

I knew there was no need in fighting about it. As far as my mom was concerned, it was a done deal. Resigned to the inevitable—no matter how embarrassing it might be—I gave in.

"Just do whatever you want to do, Mama."

Even by Mississippi Delta standards, this reception planned by my mama was "over the top." When she and Mrs. Ricks arrived in Nashville, they brought with them a white, lace tablecloth; a big silver urn of flowers; a silver punch bowl with matching cups and ladle, and a frozen fruit ring; homemade cheese straws from Ms. Gwen James; and a sheet cake from Madole's Bakery. If you got a cake from Madole's, you were considered "uptown"! Their cakes were *the best*!

You may ask how having those things made this reception "over the top." Well, when Mama brought in the Madole's sheet cake, she opened the box with an ecstatic smile on her face and cocked her head ever-so slightly at me. "Wait 'til you see this." I noticed that resting on top of the cake was a grand piano music box. Looking around to make sure no one was watching, I quietly, if not reluctantly, ambled over, lifted the lid of the piano, and to my horror, "My Way" began to play.

Of course, Mama insisted the lid stay up throughout the reception.

On the table, a big lace ribbon ran like a runner down the middle. The standard peanuts and soft mints were cast about in silver serving bowls. My mom even had napkins printed with a piano, my name, and the date of my event. And to top it all off, Mama told me, "Now be sure to invite everyone to your reception before your last song."

"Mama, I'm pretty sure they'll see it out there." Even though a reception had never followed anyone's recital in the history of the school, voicing such an invitation was sure to be frowned upon by my professors and make me the laughing stock of the music department.

At the actual recital, the audience contained many friends from the Nashville church where I attended, college professors, and other music students. At the completion of the recital, I stood up before playing my final song and welcomed my mother and Mrs. Ricks. Now, while I was very proud and grateful that Mama was there for me, I still didn't want to offer that invitation aloud. But seeing the excitement on her face as she was urging me on with the excitement of a little girl on Christmas morning, I simply had no choice. Quite sheepishly, I asked anyone who would care to stick around and join us for the reception that Mama had prepared was welcome to do so. Deep down, I believed there wouldn't be a soul there but Mama, Mrs. Ricks, maybe a professor or two, and me.

Needless to say, everyone stayed, and there wasn't a peanut, cheese straw, crust of bread, or crumb of cake left . . . and certainly no frozen fruit ring.

When it was all over and we were cleaning up, I looked over at my mom. She had been quietly working, packing up all the bowls, table-cloths, and, yes, the grand piano music box; and I was ashamed that she knew how embarrassed I was at the thought of this reception in the beginning.

"Told ya." She never looked up from her work.

I'm glad to have such a wonderful memory of my mother, who, by the way, created a lasting legacy at Belmont University. For every year since that day, just about every single student who has had a senior recital has had a reception.

CHAPTER 6

FAKE IT 'TIL YOU MAKE IT, BOY

F ROM THE TIME I WAS IN SIXTH GRADE, I KNEW I WANTED TO MAKE A living playing music. I loved performing for people, and whenever my parents had friends over for dinner, their kids and I would come up with an idea for an impromptu musical, with me directing, and we would "premiere" it by the end of the night, forcing our parents to endure our "show." Besides that, my sisters and I sang and played together many times at North Greenwood Baptist Church, as well as other smaller churches in the surrounding area. The first time I performed in front of people, I was nine years old, playing "What a Friend We Have in Jesus," while Roy Sylvester, a close family friend, preached at the Ebenezer Baptist Church in Lexington, Mississippi. I was petrified.

My first introduction into the world of "paying gigs" came when I was invited to play for the dinner hour at the Greenwood Country Club. I was thirteen, and my mama would drive me there on Fridays and Saturdays. That first night I carried with me the large green *Reader's Digest Family Songbook*—a collection of familiar old standards—that Mama had special-ordered for me because she said that those would be the songs people would want to hear. As I approached the piano, I saw two older black gentlemen sitting beside the piano with their instruments waiting on me. One had a bass guitar and the other a set of drums. "Ya'll playing, too?" I asked innocently. I had never played with adults, and certainly had never been paid, so this was all new to me.

The first couple of nights I sat down at the piano, opened the book to a particular song, and asked the men, "Do ya'll know this one?" They would just look at me like I was crazy. Finally, after a few weekends of this, the bass player couldn't take it anymore. "Boy, close that book."

"I can't close the book," I argued. "I need the music."

"Boy, close that book and scoot over." I was mesmerized because this man played with such passion, and whenever somebody could improvise in such an old bluesy style as he did, it captured me right away. I understood that kind of music, because to be able to play that way is a gift few have, but when you are blessed with it and you understand it, you respect it. From week to week, they could see that I had something in me as well, and they took me under their wing. This man played with such soul, and the chord changes and substitutions he taught me that night, and in the months that followed, impacted the way I play to this day.

"Now, son," he told me, "if someone in the crowd asks you to play a song, whatever they request, you say you know it, and you start playing."

"But what if I don't know it?"

"Well," he smiled a big, toothy smile, "you just fake it 'til you make it, boy."

I got paid $75 per night, plus tips, playing at the GCC. The men I played with recognized a novelty when they saw one and made sure they brought in a big fish bowl for the tips, because they knew that everybody would be thinking how cute it was that this young boy was playing for them. They also knew that the more drunk the customers got, the more tips we'd get, and so whenever someone came stumbling up to the piano with a song request I didn't know, I'd look at the seasoned blues musicians in panic, and the bass guitarist would simply grin and say, "He knows it."

In the meantime, Buddy the bartender would come over to me a few times a night and ask me slyly, "Wha' chu wanna drank?"

"I don't know," I innocently replied.

"I'll brang ya somethin'!"

One night he brought me some orange juice, but when I took a sip between songs, it didn't taste like any orange juice I'd ever had before. It had a little kick to it. I didn't want to be rude, so I drank it.

IN THE EARLY 1980S, TO BE COOL YOU *HAD* TO HAVE AT LEAST ONE IZOD OR Polo shirt in your closet. They were pretty expensive, so Mama opted for JC Penney's knock-off version, which had a fox instead of the Izod alligator.

"I'm not wearing that," I said. And the battle began right there in the middle of JC Penney's. It was already bad enough that we had to shop for my clothes in the "husky" section. Now to have to wear a fox on top of that? Too much.

"You'll wear it and like it!" she fired back.

"I'll cut that fox off."

"You do, and I'll cut your tail off!" It was over, and I knew I'd better let it go. Especially when she quipped, "If anybody would have ever told me. . . . "

So, with the money I made from working at the country club, my plan was to fill my closet with the very Izod and Polo shirts that Mama and Daddy wouldn't buy for me. However, they had a different plan. There was a Stein Mart store fifty miles away in Greenville that had a large bin of defective Izods and Polos that were extremely discounted, and they decided I could buy a few shirts there every now and then. The only one I could find that fit me had one sleeve shorter than the other and a headless polo man. I wore it proudly with the sleeves rolled up.

I HAD SOME GREAT PIANO TEACHERS AND MUSIC PROFESSORS IN MY LIFE, but my time with those two wonderfully talented men at the Greenwood Country Club prepared me as much as anything else to be a performer.

A year after I graduated from Belmont University, I was invited to play for "Sunday Morning Country" as part of Fan Fare Week at the Grand Ole Opry House in Nashville. The show was produced by a lady named Karen, who needed a pianist for the large choir that would sing all the great hymns while stars like Roy Acuff would come out on stage and join in.

Following that opportunity, Karen called to tell me she was organizing a concert tour to perform at the Country Night Festival in Switzerland with Loretta Lynn, Conway Twitty, and Vernon Oxford. She asked if I'd be interested in travelling as part of Vernon's band. And while Loretta and Conway were two of the biggest names in the history of country music, I have to be honest . . . I had never heard of Vernon Oxford. But when someone is extending an invitation to spend some time in the Swiss Alps, it takes all of about two seconds to say, "*Yes!*"

Being so young, I didn't know what to expect. There were a lot of "firsts" for me on that trip. At the end of a nine-hour flight to Zurich, I was picked up in a limo and driven three hours to Gstaad in the heart of the Alps.

We stayed at a place called Arc-en-Ciel ("The Rainbow"), a beautiful hotel settled within the Swiss Mountain Range, and I was given my own room, which from my experience was something completely new. I was used to rooming with five people, with some sleeping on the floor, but at the Arc-en-Ciel I thought I had won the lottery. My room was beautiful, with wooden doors that opened onto a spacious balcony that overlooked the mountains. When the windows were open, the curtains wafted in the breeze. The bed was like a big, poufy cloud of comforters, sheets, and pillows. There was a featherbed on the bottom and a down comforter on top, so that when you laid down, you were enveloped like a cocoon. I loved that bed so much that when I got home, I re-created that bed for my own bedroom. Today, "The Cloud" is in one of my guest rooms for friends and family to enjoy.

My room also had a mini bar, which I had never seen before, and the signature piece of the bathroom was a giant claw-foot bathtub. Every night I would fill the tub with water, turn on some music, and feel the autumn breeze. "This is the life," I thought.

Breakfast in Switzerland was quite different than it was in Mississippi. While I was used to grits, bacon, biscuits, and eggs, Europeans usually eat only breads, cheeses, scones, jams, and jellies for breakfast. One morning there was this huge wooden table with several large wheels of cheese. I love cheese, so this was like a smorgasbord to me.

After filling my plate, I sat down with some of the other musicians at the table and noticed a horrible smell. I looked at them. I looked under the table, then I looked all around the room before I realized the smell was coming from the middle of my plate from a mound of stinky, unpasteurized cheese staring up at me. The other guys, all seasoned travelers, knew not to touch the stuff, and thoroughly enjoyed poking fun at the "newbie." From that point on, they often made references to the keyboard player from Mississippi and his "great love of stinky cheese."

When it came time for my first show with Vernon, I was pretty excited to see that, even though no one probably knew who he was, at least there was a packed house there to see Loretta, Conway, and the Forrester

Sisters, who had met up with us once we got there. Joey Cigainero, an extremely gifted pianist, and a friend of mine from Belmont University, was playing with the Forrester Sisters.

To my amazement, when Vernon Oxford walked out on stage, I felt like I was at a Beatles concert. I'm telling you, people went crazy for him, screaming and hollering. They loved him. To say Vernon was big in Europe would be an understatement. Raised in Wichita, Kansas, he learned to play old-time fiddle from his father and at age nineteen began playing professionally. And though he got signed by RCA Victor in 1965, he was soon dropped when none of his songs charted.

But by the middle of the 1970s, European countries embraced his music, especially Great Britain, where he had hit singles from such titles as "Shadows of My Mind," "I've Got to Get Peter Off Your Mind," "Field of Flowers," and, my personal favorite, "(The Night) We Came Awfully Close to Sin."

I was in my early twenties, so at fifty-something Vernon seemed old to me. But after a few rehearsals, he was quickly becoming one of my favorite people in the world. He was a super funny guy and would do this buck dancing thing that the Europeans loved. Maybe they connected with it so much because, while it is a variation of clogging, it actually has roots from Northern Europeans who, after settling in North America, mixed their dances with African dances like the Juba. Both clogging and tap dancing derived from buck dancing. So, when Vernon began to dance, people would go crazy. They loved it, and it was part of what made him such a popular artist and endeared him to his audiences.

When we returned to the United States from that quick tour, Joey had the opportunity to play with Reba McEntire, which opened a slot to play with the Forrester Sisters. They asked me to go on tour with them, and while I was flattered that they would ask, I had already committed to go on the road with Suzy Bogguss.

I had a blast with Suzy. Again, all this traveling was new to me, but it was a great education in both music and life. We were on our way to the Hodag Festival in Wisconsin one night when the bus driver stopped and woke us up so that we could check out the Northern Lights. I'd never seen anything like it and was blown away.

I also learned that, unfortunately, even when life seems to be perfect, it's still very fragile.

On a rare weekend off, I had just walked in the door of my apartment, flipped on the television, and was shocked as I listened to a Nashville station report that a plane had crashed near the Mexican border. On that flight were the tour manager and seven members of Reba's band, including my friend Joey. All died in the wreckage. The Hawker Sidley aircraft had taken off from Brown Field, a private airport near San Diego, and went down around 1:40 a.m., after the jet's wing had clipped an outcropping of rock near the 3,572-foot peak and cartwheeled into Olay Mountain at 200 miles per hour. Reba's band had played just four hours earlier in San Diego and, ironically, the last number they played together was "Sweet Dreams," Reba's tribute to the legendary Patsy Cline, who had died in a plane crash some thirty years before. Reba, two other members of the band, and some road crew had taken off on an earlier flight and made it safely back to the East Coast.

When I saw the list of the names appear on the screen, including Joey's, tears began to roll down my face as I wondered what he must have been thinking as that plane went down. Memories of days we spent in college and the great experience of running around Switzerland together were still fresh in my mind. To this day, they are some of my fondest memories because it was such an amazing opportunity for two young musicians and friends. I immediately grabbed my box of pictures and dug out some of Joey and me when we were all together in Switzerland and eventually gave them to a buddy to pass on to Joey's parents.

Reba and Suzy were a lot alike in the way they treated the people around them. Like Reba, Suzy usually traveled on the bus with us—something stars normally don't do. And while she was such a great performer, she was like a big sister to me during the year I toured with her. There were many times when she would jam on the bus with us and laugh and sing like we all grew up together. I always looked forward to getting on the bus after a concert with her and the rest of the guys because she embraced every opportunity to simply have fun. Some people forget how to enjoy life once they get to her level of success. Suzy has never forgotten, and the time I spent with her—not to mention all the great memories—always brings a smile to my face.

One night we were on stage performing at a state fair, and Travis Tritt was coming on after us. I had bought this cool, pirate-looking shirt from a place called Dangerous Threads in Nashville. It was all white and had these poufy sleeves and oversized cuffs. I wore black jeans with brown suede chaps sown in the legs and a pair of Pieced Python boots, courtesy of the endorsement Suzy had with the Justin Boot Company. As we were walking off the stage, I noticed Travis Tritt was wearing the exact same pirate shirt, and as we crossed paths, his eyes bugged a little, then we both smiled. I winked at him and said, "Too bad, bro. They've already seen it."

As I walked down the steps to our dressing rooms, I remember feeling like a million bucks. In my heart I was loving life on the road. For sure, I could see myself doing this the rest of my life.

Until I couldn't.

CHAPTER 7

I MADE YOU FOR MORE THAN THIS

During my year with Suzy Bogguss, I came to know why she is one of the all-time greats in country music history, and not just because she achieved back-to-back gold records in the early 1990s, or because she won the Country Music Association's Horizon Award, or even because she was nominated for a Grammy Award. She's one of the all-time greats because she loves her fans, is a great singer/songwriter, and is the consummate professional. Beyond that, she is genuinely kind and a joy to be around.

Playing keyboard with her band in 1991 was a great experience during a time in my career when I needed to be on the road. Traveling with her provided a much-needed reprieve from a tumultuous stint at a church where I played in the worship band. I had attended this church for about four years before a man had come there seeking restoration after losing his ministry because of a sexual addiction.

After about three years of counseling, the senior pastor of the church wanted to give this man a chance to be restored into the ministry. He genuinely felt three years was long enough to deal with the issues that caused his downfall and nearly cost him his family. One of the stipulations for him to be able to go out again in a ministerial capacity was that someone had to accompany him as an accountability partner. One weekend, the young man appointed to be with him was unavailable, so I was asked to lead worship for the event where he was speaking. As we traveled, he was very open about his journey through abuse and subsequent addiction, and it was the first time I had heard someone be so transparent about these kinds of issues. I even felt comfortable sharing some of my own experiences of abuse when I was a child.

We checked in at the hotel, and the next morning we were to do the first of two events that day. After the morning session, we returned to the hotel for the afternoon to rest for the later event. I had gone back to my room when he called and asked me to come to his room for a minute. When he tried to seduce me into having an "encounter" with him, I was stunned and got away from him as quickly as I could. I didn't know anybody there, so I really didn't know how to handle this incident. I can't begin to describe how difficult it was to lead a congregation of people in worship knowing this man was going to follow me and preach.

To my amazement, a few days after we arrived back home, he went to the pastor and the leadership of the church and told them that I "had a problem." The church took me out of every leadership position that I had, and refused to listen to my side of the story when they called me into the office to talk about the incident. By the end of the week, the Lord had led me to contact a professional counselor.

So, needless to say, I look back and see that God was pulling me away from that situation by opening a door to travel with Suzy. It was just the Lord's amnesty because nobody on the tour knew what was going on with me there, and I needed that safe place in my life.

I was traveling the world playing at amazing venues, in front of huge crowds, and meeting a lot of country music's most popular artists. This tour seemed to be taking me everywhere I had wanted to be my entire life. At one particular concert in Lake Charles, Louisiana, we were doing a show with Ricky Van Shelton and Alabama, at that time two of the most popular country music acts in the world. The arena was packed with about 30,000 people, and I got my moment in the spotlight with a piano solo. I remember thinking, *This is awesome! I'm living the dream!*

While I was under the spotlight and the audience was cheering, I felt a rush of adrenaline . . . I was getting lost in the moment. All those years of tuba and piano lessons and playing for dinner hours were finally paying off. At that moment, there wasn't anything in the world that could have made me happier.

Yet, somewhere in the middle of that solo, it was like someone had hit the mute button, and the crowd began to move in slow motion all around me almost like a Hollywood dream sequence. I felt like I was enclosed in a bubble, and I could sense the Lord telling me, *This is what you thought you always wanted . . . but, I made you for more than this.*

It was only three years after I had graduated from Belmont University, and here I was thinking I had fulfilled everything I wanted. I had traveled internationally, was writing music, and was now playing for one of the darlings of country music in front of thousands. Yet now I found myself thinking, *I'm a side man in a country band. Am I really doing something that matters? What real difference am I making with the gift God gave me?*

I learned a very valuable lesson in that moment: Sometimes it takes time for God to reveal something that's better for us than what we have in mind for ourselves.

The whole nature of the music business is that there is constant change. And many times after a tour concludes, the star performers will change things up within their bands. Because there are no real long-term guarantees, you're never really settled.

After that year with Suzy, she brought in a whole new band, so I went back to teaching piano and voice lessons full-time. In August 1993, I was asked to play piano while prospective backup singers and musicians auditioned for an upcoming tour with Kenny Rogers. By then, Kenny was a world-renowned star, having already had two of his albums (*The Gambler* and *Kenny*) named in the About.com poll of "The 200 Most Influential Country Albums Ever." In a 1986 poll, he was named "The Favorite Singer of All Time" by readers of both *USA Today* and *People Magazine*.

The tour's producer and I hit it off and were discussing some of the singers who had auditioned one day. Every single one of them was either from New York or Chicago, and they were all singing these big, dramatic ballads. While they were great singers, the songs began to blend together, and our ears got numb listening to the same thing over and over.

As we talked through the strengths and weaknesses of each one, the producer said, "Why don't you audition to go on the tour?"

"Because you're not paying enough," I shot back. I wasn't being a diva, but the truth was that I could stay home teaching lessons and pay all my bills. That wasn't the case for what they were paying those going on the tour.

"Well, just play and sing something for me."

As a joke, I started slamming out a fun rendition of James Brown's Motown hit "I Feel Good" and was really just cuttin' up and having fun. It was a complete contrast to what we'd been listening to for hours, and he absolutely loved it. "You've got to go with us," he insisted.

"I really can't," I responded. "I couldn't make it on what ya'll are paying. I make more teaching, so I have to stay here. I can't take a cut in pay."

"What would it take for you to go?"

Just off the top of my head I threw out three stipulations that it would take for me to leave the fifty-six students a week I was teaching at the time.

He didn't even bat an eye. "Okay. Done."

"Okay. When do we leave?"

During the six-week Christmas tour in 1993, we played forty-two shows. We would play a segment of Christmas songs, Kenny would do some of his greatest hits, then we'd finish with more Christmas favorites. In the process, we consistently packed 5,000- to 15,000-seat auditoriums and arenas all over the Midwest and eastern side of the country.

We were on *Entertainment Tonight* one time, and I was sitting next to Kenny during the interview. I didn't get to say anything, but Daddy saw me on TV at home, and it was the first time he actually believed I could make a living at this music thing after all.

But God showed me something more during that tour. He further taught me that something else was coming into my life, because He put me on that tour with Kenny for no other reason than to see what kind of toll years on the road can take. Most of the band members had been with Kenny for thirty years or more, and as I watched them over those weeks, I would find myself wondering, *Is this what I really want to do?*

To be sure, these guys made a lot of money, but they were rarely with their families. They traveled most the time and missed many of those "moments" that are so important. God opened my eyes and began to place a different desire in my heart, even if I wasn't sure what it was at that time.

When the tour ended and I got home on Christmas Eve, it was only a couple of months later that my song "One More Broken Heart" went to #1 for Point of Grace. I wrote some songs for Integrity Music for a while after that, building what I hoped to be an attractive portfolio to further my career in the Nashville music scene. Even when I was with Suzy and Kenny on tour, I was writing kids music and would be asked to do camps and play at churches. Then I got the call that would change everything for me.

"Someone recommended that we should call you and see if you'd be interested in writing VBS music for us," Lynne Norris from LifeWay told me over the phone. I had met Lynne through her father, Don, who was a music minister in Nashville.

"VBS? Like Vacation Bible School VBS? Like all over the country VBS?"

"That's the one."

"Of course I'd be interested." And I was. After all, only a week before I had played a gig at a VFW club for a bunch of toothless drunks clamoring for me to "Play some Con-wayyyy!" and thought I'd hit rock-bottom.

"Good," she said. "Bring us a tape."

I took them a cassette tape that day (it was 1996, after all) and Lynne called less than twenty-four hours later. "We'd love for you to write our VBS music. The only thing is we'll need all the songs by the twentieth."

"Of August?"

"Yes."

"Today's the fifth."

"I know," she said with a sigh. "It's a long story."

As it turned out, LifeWay had completely revamped its VBS and was now facing a small window of time to complete the following year's

VBS packet, including all the music, which incorporated the theme song and five daily songs. They had started in August and had until the end of October to do what normally takes two years. There were people literally sleeping in their offices and staying through weekends, trying to get every detail covered, every Bible study written, every craft planned, and every mission lesson completed. The VBS department was on life support and was literally "going under." It had developed a program called "The Highway to Happiness," and it was in the warehouse ready to ship.

Bill Taylor, who was head of the department at that time, made the decision to throw it all away and start over. "We've got to do something different," he surmised. That something was "The Wild and Wonderful Good News Stampede."

My part in all this was to write the six songs. I had written musicals before, but really didn't have an idea of what they needed. So, in my first venture with LifeWay, I made a big blunder. I assumed that, as in other musicals, the number of songs could fluctuate. I mean, really, is there that much difference between five or six songs? So, I just wrote five thinking, *These are pretty good. I think they can make it with five.*

When it came time to present them to the team, I sang the songs I had written. They liked them, and we started talking about production ideas. "Oh, we haven't heard the Day Two song yet," they said as we were wrapping up.

"I didn't have time to write it."

Panic ensued, and they started clucking about like chickens, wondering how we could possibly live without a Day Two song. So, that night I went home and wrote "Closer Than You Think."

During that time I followed the lead of that determined team of writers and developers and stayed up basically for fifteen days and nights. The lack of rest, along with the amount of stress, caused me to get run-down. I developed bacterial pharyngitis, a painful, strep-like disease of the throat. Little did I realize, we were just getting started.

Now that LifeWay had "Stampede" in the can, we were in catch-up mode and needed to write two more VBS programs by the end of 1997. In February we began work on "Star Quest Galactic Good News Adventure," and just a few months after completing that one, we started on "Mount Extreme: The Ultimate Good News Challenge."

In one crazy year's time, we wrote three full Vacation Bible School programs. But God truly blessed the efforts. The response to "Stampede" was immediate and strong, and helped a flailing VBS department get back on its feet and begin to thrive. While the response increased over the next three years, by 2000 to 2001, the growth was exponential, and LifeWay became known worldwide for its VBS programs as much as anything else it produced.

When we did "Stampede," the motions that go with the songs were printed in the back of the musical score, as they always had been. I stood in front of a lady named Kay Parker and would demonstrate all the motions as she tried her best to translate on paper what she was seeing. Needless to say, Kay and I became very close friends. The directions had little cartoon characters demonstrating the moves, with swirly arrows showing the direction the arms, legs, and heads were supposed to swing and rotate. Each motion had a corresponding number that, in turn, corresponded with a number in the music where the motion was supposed to occur. I'm sure people got dizzy trying to figure it all out and make sure the motions matched the words of the songs.

In 1998, the Lord gave me the idea to do a video where I would demonstrate the motions and make it a lot easier for people. I told Lynne about my idea. "We don't have any budget for that."

"We don't need a budget," I responded. "Just get a camera and let me stand up and do it."

So that first video we shot for "Mount Extreme" was recorded in Van Ness Auditorium at the LifeWay building. The only "props" we had were a few borrowed sleeping bags scattered around the stage and a LifeWay banner hanging on a stand behind me. The video was met with rave reviews. It made teaching the motions to church VBS leaders so much easier to understand and, in turn, easier for them to teach the children in their respective churches during their week of Vacation Bible School.

The Lord gave me a specific vision in how I was to record these videos. It needed to feel as if I were in their homes teaching them these motions one-on-one in their living rooms. I wanted to share stories behind the songs and how they were written to give people ownership in them. I didn't want to worry about being perfect, so if I messed up, I just laughed it off and kept going. It was all about honoring the Lord by not being perfect, but by doing my best to worship and enjoy spending time with Him . . . and passing that on to all the kids who would eventually learn these same motions.

The videos were real and personable, and we had a blast doing them. I think in large part this was something that made the music side of VBS so successful. From its humble beginnings on that stage in Van Ness Auditorium, we eventually shot videos all over the world, including Australia, Israel, Colorado, and Hawaii. I am humbled by the fact that these DVDs went triple platinum and more than 150,000 copies were sold over that time.

In 1999, a youth minister I had worked with at a Kentucky Changers event named Andy McDonald wanted to introduce me to a trio of brothers in Henderson, Kentucky. He said they were pretty talented musicians, even if they were young, and thought it would be a good idea for them to play with me while I was there in Henderson doing a concert.

"The Durbin brothers are well known around here," he promised. Their names were Jonathon, Wesley, and Todd.

"How old are they?" I asked.

"Jonathon's twenty-one, Wesley is eighteen, and Todd is fifteen."

"Fifteen?"

"Yeah, but he's really talented," he promised.

I thought, *Well, whatever. Let's see what happens.* What I didn't know was that their mother was a worship leader and had raised them to play and flow. Not only were they truly talented; they were truly anointed. They jumped right in with me, and it was a comfortable fit right away. I loved playing with them while I was there, and I told them that I just knew there was more for us to do together, but had no idea what it was . . . until I met Randy Hall.

By the time Randy approached me in 1999, he had nurtured his vision and passion for Student Life camps for seven years and was ready to add children's camps to the Student Life family. He wanted to host the first Student Life for Kids Camp in the summer of 2000 and wanted me to lead worship for them.

"But," he added, "if you do the camps, you'll need a band."

I knew exactly who to call. When I made contact with the Durbins, Wesley was the one who called me back. He apparently appointed himself their "business manager" and promised to talk it over with his brothers as well as their parents, Dennis and Sue, and get back with me.

About fifteen minutes later my phone rang. "We really, really want to do this," he said, and I could tell in his voice he was anxious about something. "The only thing is, Jeff, how much will we need to pay to do this?"

"What?" I asked. "You don't pay anything. I pay you and take care of your expenses."

"Aw, that's great! We'll be glad to do it, then."

I laughed as I put the phone down, and I knew then, without a doubt, I had the right group. They were so humble and possessed true servant hearts. Those brothers loved leading kids in worship, and the kids were crazy about them.

I will never forget that summer, for several reasons. There were moments with kids that changed my life. So many times, worship leaders play, sing, and then leave. But at camp you can eat, hang out, and spend some real quality time with kids. It doesn't take them long to figure out that you care about them. I don't always understand the rapport the Lord gives me with kids, but I thank Him every day for it, because it's a precious gift. Over the years, I've had kids email me to say, "You were a big part of my spiritual growth."

A crowd of 30,000 people in an arena in Lake Charles is a long way from a small auditorium with 1,000 kids, but during that first summer of Student Life for Kids Camp, I remember a twelve-year-old girl walking up to me just after worship. Tears were streaming down her cheeks, and she said, "I felt God for the first time tonight."

"Really?"

"Yeah," she said, almost in a whisper. "My daddy died when I was little, and I've always felt strange because all of my friends have daddies and I don't. But tonight I felt the Lord tell me that I don't have to feel like that anymore because He's my Daddy."

With her words ringing in my head and my heart overwhelmed by what had just transpired, I sat quietly on the stage and watched the kids file out of the auditorium. I could feel the Lord saying to me, *This is it. This is what I made you for.*

CHAPTER 8

SUN ON MY FACE

W HEN I DECIDED TO WRITE SOME OF THE STORIES FROM MY LIFE, I looked forward to sharing all the experiences God has blessed me with. I couldn't wait to talk about my mama, or how the Lord redeemed the relationship with my dad, or about losing my sweet fourteen-year-old niece Mallorie, or the great memories of friends and others I've worked with, and stories that have kept my family laughing for years. But, to be honest, I knew my story wouldn't be complete if I didn't talk about the heart-breaking and shameful sexual abuse I suffered for more than six years at the hands of my great uncle.

To be sure, this was the part of my life that I dreaded talking about the most.

But it's also the story of an important turning point in my life, when I was finally able to take the first steps in fulfilling God's calling. I hope that by telling this story, I might encourage others who have experienced similar horrific acts.

When God said to me, *I made you for more than this*, He also meant that He made me for more than I thought I was worth.

My daddy's grandmother lived in a small house in Sumner, Mississippi, and we would spend some time every summer visiting her. She had this one bedroom that was my favorite room in the house because it had a clear view of her land, and at just the perfect time of day, the sun would shine through and hit the glass at just the right angle, so that you could literally see the beams of light filling up the room.

I don't remember the first time my great uncle abused me sexually. But there was one day—I must have been about five—when he came into that room and shut the door. When he walked over and picked me up to sit down in the rocking chair with him, I knew what was going to happen.

The rocking chair was sitting near the window. Fortunately, my main memory of that afternoon was turning my face toward that window and squinting my eyes as hard as I could to try and focus on the warmth of the sun on my face. I now realize the irony of the light coming in to battle against the darkness that was enveloping me in that room. Before he walked out, he told me, as he had before, "Don't say anything to anybody, because you know if your daddy finds out, he'll be mad at you, and he'll whip you."

I was eleven years old the last time it happened. He was staying with us in our home in Greenwood, sleeping on our living room couch. My sisters and one of their boyfriends were downstairs in the den, and I tried to stay up as late as possible with them. But they eventually sent me up to my room. I tried as best I could not to make a sound as I walked through the dining room, through the kitchen, and down the short hallway to my room. I wanted at all costs to avoid any possible exchange with him. My hope was that he was already asleep. Once I got to my room, I shut the door as quietly as I could. There was no lock.

I got in bed with rattled nerves and hoped against hope he hadn't heard me. But that hope faded when I heard the creaking of the floor as he slowly walked down the hallway. My heart started racing. Then the door knob began to turn. I pulled the covers all around me, pretending to be asleep as I lay on the top of my bunk bed, but I could feel him standing beside my bed staring at me. Then he sat down on the bottom bunk and lay down. I waited a long time, trying to formulate a plan to get out of the room. If I could just get to the end of my bed, I thought, I could jump down and beat him to the bathroom. Unlike my bedroom door, the bathroom door had a lock, and I could keep him away from me.

I could hear him breathing, and I began to think he had fallen asleep. But as soon as my feet hit the floor, he grabbed me. I refused to give in to him, and when he pulled me onto the bottom bunk, I fought my way free and made it to the safety of the bathroom.

Mama heard me throwing up behind the locked door. She wanted me to let her in because she thought I had the flu. Meanwhile, my great uncle had run back to the living room to his couch. When I let her in, my mother put a cold cloth on my head to make me feel better. I looked up at her pleadingly, "Can I sleep with you and Daddy tonight?"

FIFTEEN YEARS LATER, AFTER EVERYTHING HAD BLOWN UP AT THE CHURCH where I had served for four years, I was supposed to meet with a publisher friend named John and do some writing for him. But, obviously, I was in no shape to do anything, let alone write music on that blustery January afternoon.

"Bro, what's wrong with you?" John asked me.

"I can't tell you," I said. "But I need you to tell me something. When you hear my name, what do you think?" I'm sure he was taken aback by such a weird question, but I told him, "I can't tell you what's going on, but I feel like I'm having a breakdown and I just need to know what kind of person you think I am." John was very encouraging to me, and described me as a person who gave a lot of himself and loved people. I didn't realize at the time that he had been through some similar things in his childhood and was on his own journey through healing. He and I had become friends a few years before, and he had signed me right out of college to write songs for the publishing company he worked for.

"I've never had a breakdown, so I'm not sure what it's like," I told him. "But I feel like I'm about to have one."

"If you need to talk to someone, I know a counselor you can call. I've actually been going to him for a while myself," John replied. He wrote down the number for Dr. John Abney, who worked at a place called Positive Horizons. He said that Dr. Abney charged $75 per session, but it really didn't matter what he charged, because I didn't know if I'd ever call that number. In 1991, nobody ever went to see a counselor, unless they were "crazy."

Before I decided whether or not to call Dr. Abney, the first thing I wanted to do was drive to Franklin and sit in Minerva's kitchen. When she opened the door, she could tell by the look on my face that something terrible had happened. "What's wrong?" she asked me tenderly. I walked slowly to the kitchen table and sat down. "I need to tell you a long story." I proceeded to tell her everything, from my childhood abuse to what had just transpired at the church. All through that weekend, Minerva loved on me, encouraged me, and prayed for me. I felt so safe with her.

Afterward, I decided to call Dr. Abney and make an appointment, though I did so with great fear. Before I hung up, I summoned the courage to say awkwardly, "I'm not crazy."

There was a hearty chuckle on the other end of the phone. "Oh Jeff, we're all 'crazy,'" Dr. Abney responded.

On my way to the first session, I started wondering how I was going to pay for counseling. I didn't know how often I'd have to go, and if this stretched out over several months, there was no way I could afford it; I was financially treading water as it was. "Lord," I said, "if this is something you want me to do, then I'll do it, but You have to make a way for me to be able to afford it."

The first session began typically enough, with Dr. Abney asking me some general questions. After going down his list, he said out of the blue, "Well, Jeff, the first thing we need to do is deal with the issues with your dad."

"What? My dad? I don't have any issues with my daddy. I can't stand him, and I'm okay with that."

"Exactly."

"Dr. Abney, I feel like I need to be honest with you. I know you can probably help me," I said, changing the subject, "but I'm not really sure I can afford it."

"I actually charge on a sliding scale," he said. "Take this piece of paper and write down your expenses and what you make each month, and we'll decide your fee."

I wrote it all down, and he looked at it. "Do you think you could do $20 a week?"

"Yeah, I can do that." I was shocked. "But you'll do it for that?"

"Yes, $20 will be your fee."

I was able to see Dr. Abney for sixteen months. He was a terrific counselor, and I loved the fact that he used scripture in his sessions. When I told him that I felt like damaged goods and wondered if anyone would ever want me, he said, "You know, Jeff, you are fearfully and wonderfully made," referring to Psalm 139. This was a passage I was very familiar with, thanks to Minerva.

One day, Dr. Abney told me to draw three pictures. One was to be a self-portrait; the second, a sketch of me and my family doing something together; and the third, a drawing of me, a tree, and a house.

For the first one, I drew only my face. "I'm not a good artist," I said, but that didn't really matter. For the second picture, I drew my family and me sitting around the table eating supper. In the third, I drew a house with a fountain in the front yard. Then I drew me sitting on the edge of the fountain dangling my feet over the water.

When he looked at the self-portrait, he asked me, "Why didn't you draw a body for yourself?"

"I'm not good at drawing bodies." Then I offered several lame excuses.

"Do you think you didn't draw your body because you may be 'ashamed' of your body?"

His words hit me like a slap in the face. They were a revelation as I was able to make the connection to my subconscious feelings. "Well, I never thought of that before."

Then he looked at the family drawing. He began to describe my family and noticed I had drawn myself sitting next to my mother. "You're closer to your mom," he said matter-of-factly. "But your dad is very protective and likes to have the whole family around him. He wants to keep you all under his umbrella. That's why you're all around a table. He would probably prefer that you never moved away from home."

I was amazed at his accuracy in describing my family from a simple picture. He was spot-on.

Then he came to the final sketch. "Oh, my," he said.

"What?"

"I didn't tell you to draw a fountain."

"I know. I just wanted to draw a mansion and have a fountain." My attempt at nervous humor was awkward.

"Jeff, I want you to look at the fountain and tell me what it looks like to you." I didn't realize what I had drawn, but something within me was trying to reveal to Dr. Abney what I wasn't aware I was divulging. I won't go into detail about what my subconscious drew on that paper, but it revealed that I had issues with intimacy, or so Dr. Abney said. "Jeff, you're dangling your feet over the edge of the fountain, but you won't jump in. You won't commit. Why wouldn't you draw yourself playing in the fountain? To me, this fountain represents intimacy, and you have a fear of committing to that."

And that was how the sessions went. The emotions that came up were raw and deep, but necessary if I wanted to heal.

From there, we dealt with my feelings about my dad. I told him how my daddy wanted a huntin', fishin', football-playin', tobacco-spittin', rough-and-tumble Mississippi Delta boy, and I didn't know how to be what he wanted.

"You know, Jeff, God didn't make a mistake by making him your father," Dr. Abney told me. "There are reasons He put you two together."

Until then, I had this one-dimensional view of my dad. He was stern, he was angry, and he allowed no room for error. I was always scared of him. While I was releasing parts of myself I had never opened up before, more and more layers began to unfold, and I discovered there were more dimensions to my father than I had ever realized.

During my many visits with Dr. Abney, he encouraged me to talk to my parents about my counseling and the issues behind it. But I wasn't there yet. In fact, I honestly didn't know when I'd be able to open up to them about something like this.

Nearly six months after I started seeing Dr. Abney, in June 1991, my sister, Vickie, and her four children came to visit me. One night, I felt that if I could practice telling Vickie about what our great uncle did to me, it would make it easier for me to tell Mama and Daddy. So, we left the kids at the house, and Vickie and I went out to dinner. At the restaurant I told her I had to share something with her. I told her it was pretty serious, and I knew I needed to tell Mama and Daddy, but I wanted to practice on her first. After I told her about the events of my childhood, she was devastated.

"So many things make sense about you now," she said through her tears. "You always had a nervous stomach, and if things weren't perfect, or you messed up, you got all out of whack."

I made Vickie promise not to tell our parents. "Don't say anything to them. I'll tell them when I'm ready."

After she returned home, Mama and Daddy knew Vickie was upset about something. Her house was just behind our parents', so they saw each other often. Her demeanor revealed to my parents that something was terribly wrong. They asked her about it until, after three days, she finally broke down and told them everything my great uncle had done. When she finished, Daddy freaked out. "I don't ever want to talk about this again. I don't want to hear his name spoken in this house again."

As it turned out, it was probably best that Vickie did tell them, because in all truth, I don't know how long it would have taken me to gather the courage to do it myself.

"DO YOU FEEL GUILTY ABOUT WHAT HAPPENED WITH YOUR GREAT UNcle?" Dr. Abney asked me in one of our sessions.

"Yes. And I've always felt like it was my fault," I replied.

"Why do you think it was your fault?"

"I guess because my daddy wasn't affectionate toward me growing up, and when my great uncle began to hug me when I was little, it was something I needed. But when it got to the point of abuse, I felt like I had caused it by allowing him to show affection toward me to start with." My mind went back to all those times he had manipulated me and had me convinced that what was going on was because of me. And I knew that I was not the only one this was happening to. My grandmother kept a box full of family pictures. Included were snapshots my great uncle had given her of him and other little boys hanging out at his house. I remember thinking, *I bet he's doing the same thing to them.*

"But you were only five years old." Dr. Abney's voice was compassionate. "It was not your fault, Jeff. You did nothing to cause him to do what he did."

When he asked me whether I had told my parents about the counseling, I told him about what had happened with Vickie, and that now they knew everything. I was able to talk to my mother about it, but I knew any communication about this with my father would have to come in the form of a letter. I wrote him one for his birthday, in which I tried to explain everything. I included the episode when my great uncle was staying at our house and Mama found me in the bathroom. I asked Daddy if he remembered my wanting to sleep with him and Mama that night. He did, because I was never the kind of kid who asked to sleep with his parents, so that night was indelibly etched in his memory.

Later, I wrote a song called "Sun on My Face," and after I recorded it, I took it home to play for Mama. The last verse of the song tells of the faith I had that God would heal that painful past:

> *There is a room in my grandmother's house*
> *Where I used to go to play*
> *There is a rocking chair there by the window*
> *Where the sun used to shine on my face.*
> *One day a man of my own family*
> *Carried me off to the room*
> *And he took me down in that chair by the window*
> *And shattered the world that I knew*
> *As we rocked, we rocked all day*
> *We rocked, oh we rocked*
>
> *And all I could feel was the sun on my face*
> *I lost myself in the warmth that it gave*
> *With nowhere to run to and nowhere to hide*
> *I clenched my eyes as my innocence died*
> *And all I could feel was the sun on my face*
>
> *Years have passed since I've been back at that house*
> *But a part of me had always remained*
> *A terrified child trapped in memories past*

Never escaping the pain
But there is a freedom that's found in truth
That breaks down the walls of our fear
Sustaining us through man's most evil intentions
And cleansing the heart with tears
In the light, the truth is revealed
In the light of the truth I am healed

And I can still feel the sun on my face
I find myself in the warmth of God's grace
When there's nowhere to run to and nowhere to hide
I close my eyes and find peace inside
'Cause I can still feel the sun on my face

While I played the recording of the song, Mama sat so still and so quiet, and tears streamed down her cheeks. At the end of it, she looked up at me, and all she could say was, "This just makes me so sad."

I wanted to put the song on my very first CD, but not without the blessing of both Mama and Daddy. I didn't want to embarrass them or make life awkward for them in their own town. "Jeff, if you think it will help people, you have our blessing."

When something as traumatic as sexual abuse happens to you, and you've bottled it up inside for so long, it's difficult to unscrew the lid on the past and just let it out. Before I could even tell Vickie, Dr. Abney had to help me to learn how to articulate those episodes. Needless to say, it was excruciating.

One day he put a teddy bear in the chair and said, "This is your great uncle. Tell him how you feel about what he did to you."

I looked at the bear, then back at Dr. Abney and began to laugh. "This is dumb. I'm not going to talk to a stuffed bear."

He continued to gently coach me into a conversation with the teddy bear, and I began to unscrew that lid little by little on my past. By the end of the session I had yelled and screamed and was on the floor in a heap sobbing. That day marked the first time I had ever vocalized the details of what transpired in those encounters with my great uncle, and every emotion I had toward him—fear, pain, embarrassment, hatred, self-loathing—all of it came out.

While I lay on the floor, mentally and emotionally spent, I noticed that Dr. Abney had become unusually quiet. When I looked up at him, I saw that he was crying, too. His tenderness toward me and that situation will be a treasure I will always carry in my heart. As he walked me to my car, he gently put his hand on my shoulder and said, "You're going to be all right."

"I know." That day had turned a corner for me.

A few months later, after Dr. Abney had helped me work through my issues with the church, then the issues with my father, it was obvious I was coming to the place where, with his help, I was able to move beyond my past.

The Lord had used Dr. Abney to help me hear His voice calling me to move from victim to victor. I sensed the Lord telling me that He had greater things in store, but until I could "cast my cares on Him," I would never find freedom from past hurts and be able to move forward. During my time with such a wonderful Christian counselor who led me through God's Word, I was able to find that healing and freedom.

In April 1992, sixteen months after I first sought his help, Dr. Abney looked at me one day with a smile. "You think you're about ready to fly?" he asked softly.

"I think so."

"I think so, too."

As I walked out of his office that afternoon, I stood by my car and closed my eyes to soak in what God had done for me during my time with Dr. Abney. As I felt the warmth of the April sun on my face, once again his words came back to me. But this time it was not him saying them. It was the familiar voice of the One who fearfully and wonderfully made me.

And He was assuring me, *You're going to be all right.*

CHAPTER 9

FILLING AN EMPTY INKWELL

IN MAY 1995 I WAS IN A REALLY NUMB PLACE, AND IT SEEMED TO ME that it had been a long time since I had felt the presence of God. I had released "Sun on My Face," had been through counseling with Dr. Abney, and had a bitter taste in my mouth from a tumultuous four-year stint at a church in Nashville. And even though I had moved on to play at Brentwood Baptist, I was mired down in a place where I didn't trust church, and it was difficult for me to connect with God.

To be honest, I was living day to day just going through the motions. While my heart hardened, though, God was working His plan and was about to unfold another chapter for me in a way I could never have imagined. New Song Church in Nashville was taking a worship band to Korea to play for the Global Conference on World Evangelism, and asked me to go along. The conference itself represented a cross-section of the world worshipping together, with 5,000 people from more than 200 different countries represented.

The event was held at a place in Seoul called The Torch Center. It was a beautiful facility where world evangelism is at the heart of its mission. The organization has been around for more than thirty years and is expanding throughout the world, raising up nation after nation with the Gospel of Christ.

The building itself was amazing. Every single room in The Torch Center was named after a fruit of the Holy Spirit. There was Love Hall, Joy Hall—which, fittingly, served as the worship center—and the Peace and Patience Press Rooms (can't help but laugh at that one). After a day of eating kimchi and sushi, I personally labeled the restroom the Long-Suffering Room—but I'll get to that later.

The most appropriately named room in the whole building, though, was found in the basement. It was called the Intercession Room. What made the name and location so strategic was that the foundation of the building housed the prayer room. The groundwork of everything done at The Torch Center is built on the power of intercessory prayer.

There wasn't anything particularly noticeable about the Intercession Room aesthetically. It was a big, round room with white cinderblock walls. It housed smaller rooms off the main room that would most closely be described as those used for Sunday School. There were no pictures to adorn the walls, and the whole setup reminded me of my childhood days at North Greenwood Baptist Church, where Mr. Granville Martin and Mr. Fred Burke would teach a group of boys lessons from God's Word and warn us *every* week to not fall prey to the worldly mind-set of "if it feels good, do it." But when this Torch Center room was fully occupied, you could close your eyes and hear the beautiful hush of people praying.

Every room in The Torch Center had staff workers and volunteers, so it was no surprise to walk into the Intercession Room and find it full of people with name tags. What separated this room from all the rest was that these people did nothing but pray during the entire conference.

From the beginning to the end, all they did was eat, sleep, and pray. That was their ministry. If no conference attendee was there, they prayed; when one walked in, several people would surround him or her and pray specifically for that person.

It was a powerful place where you could feel the presence of the Holy Spirit throughout the room.

When we first arrived in Korea after a thirty-six-hour trip, our schedule allowed us time for a quick breakfast and nap before our sound check. Standing in the breakfast line, I noticed several large, stainless steel containers like something you'd see at a "meat-and-three" buffet. These containers held something that looked like fish but not the good ol' Southern, deep-fried variety. And certainly there were no cheese grits to accompany the fish, which were raw, whole, and complete with heads, eyes, fins, and tails. For sides, there was a white root mixture, a bowl of soup, and kimchi, a fermented vegetable that had been, I was told, seasoned in a jar and buried in the ground over time. While it was pretty spicy, I really liked it. But I couldn't tell you how the fish tasted. In fact, I was about to ask someone where a Mississippi Delta boy could find the bacon and biscuit line.

But before I dishonored my Korean brothers, I spotted a street vendor who sold coffee and toast just outside the conference center doors along the bustling street, and that's where I went every day for breakfast. That little old man and I became BFF's that week, despite the fact our obvious language barrier prevented any meaningful conversation. He had no idea what "ya'll" meant. Still, no one ate more toast from his cart than I did that week.

We wanted to go to The Torch Center to get a feel for things before the conference started, but before we could, we had to officially check in at the adjoining hotel. I was sharing a room with our bass player, Mark. The room had linoleum floors from the 1970s with brown and yellow octagons and these ornate windows overlooking meticulously kept Japanese gardens with lots of bamboo and Bonzai trees, and birds that chirped constantly (even at three o'clock in the morning, we would later find out).

There was, however, no furniture. Japanese screen doors divided the room into separate sleeping quarters. We also noticed there was no closet, and in the corner of the room lay a stack of futons. We wondered why there were six futons and only two of us, but it became obvious that the hotel staff provided us with three futons each for the closest thing to a "Tempur-Pedic" experience they could match. We thought this was brilliant.

Mark and I were stacking our futons and getting settled in the room when our drummer, Stephen, walked in. We looked at him. "You're in here, too?"

"Uh . . . yeah?"

No problem, we could deal with just two futons apiece. But then another band member walked in, and he was followed by two Japanese guys we'd never seen before. And now, Mark and I had the answer to our question about the futons. Six futons for six men rather than just for the two of us. Turns out, we were all staying in this room together. Customer service indeed.

Now six men in a room can make for one awkward situation, and more so when all six futons were spread out on the floor. There wasn't even room for our suitcases. There had to have been a mistake. At least that was what I was hoping when I volunteered to go to the front desk.

"I think there's been some kind of mistake?" I proceeded to explain our dilemma to the hotel clerk.

"Sir, if you lay the futons out just right, there is room enough for everybody."

"Yes, there is," I replied. "We did that, but there is no room for our suitcases."

"You can put them in the hallway." Just as I was about to reply, he added. "Now, brother, you've got to have a missionary spirit."

"Oh, I have that," I replied, as sweet and Southern Baptist as I could. "But I would have to have a magician-ary spirit to get everyone and their stuff to fit in that room."

THE EVENING BEFORE THE CONFERENCE STARTED, WE WERE INVITED TO go to the Intercession Room. The leadership staff wanted to give the intercessors an opportunity to pray over all the worship teams. The moment we walked into the room, they came up and began to surround us to pray.

One man made eye contact with me as soon as I stepped into the room, and he walked right over. "When you walked in the door," he said, "I saw a vision of a white robe falling over you, and there was a banner over you that said, 'New Beginning, Fresh Start.' Does that mean anything to you?"

For a minute, I was awestruck, but confirmed to him that it did mean something. I was so jaded at the time. I was looking for something new when I went to New Song Church, and the Lord knew my heart did need a new beginning, a fresh start. "I think it may be the reason I am here."

ITAEWON STREET IS KNOWN ALL OVER THE WORLD FOR ITS SHOPPING AND its restaurants. Its origins date back to the early 1970s, when the United States set up a military base close by and many foreigners stationed at the base eventually settled in the Itaewon area. It is well regarded as the most exotic place in Seoul, and following the 1988 Olympics its popularity soared.

Carl Lucero and I wanted to go to Itaewon on our day off. Carl, who sang and played percussion on our team, met me in the lobby, and we formulated a game plan to get to Itaewon, shop and eat lunch, and spend the day soaking in the culture. We went to the clerk at the front desk to make sure we had directions to get back to the hotel. We knew all we had to say to the cab driver was "Itaewon" and he would take us there. The clerk took a card from her desk and wrote what we thought were the directions back to the Torch Center. I was confident we had communicated with her well enough to have no problems.

Itaewon was all it was projected to be. We had gotten a card in our welcome packet that described the market area in that region, and I knew we had to go. It was an incredible day experiencing a taste of a different way of life and being able to embrace the opportunities to figure out how to communicate with the people. When I watch *The Amazing Race* now my mind often goes back to that experience.

I've traveled all over the world, yet the language characters in Asian countries make directional signs super difficult to figure out sometimes. So, when it was time to head back, we found a cab and handed the driver the card the hotel clerk had given us. After a while, we noticed the driver was traveling in the opposite direction. Eventually, he stopped at the entrance to the Olympic Stadium.

We pleaded with the driver, "No! Torch Center! Torch Center!"

"Out!" He shouted back.

We had no choice but to leave the cab and try to find someone who spoke English to help us. But nobody would even look at us.

It was 9:00 p.m., we couldn't read any signs, we had no number for the hotel, no one spoke English, and cell phones were not yet widely used. Obviously, The Torch Center wasn't as well-known as we thought. "Carl," I said, "we are officially street people."

Finally, we spotted a subway, walked underground, and found a map with English subtitles. My eyes widened as I saw the word "Yangjae." In the midst of all this, the Lord must have felt sorry for us, because all of a sudden I remembered seeing "Yangjae-Dong" written on something at the hotel. I looked at Carl again, this time more hopeful. "Yangjae! Maybe that's close to Dong." Earlier in the week we had eaten at a TGI Fridays that was next to a subway station near our hotel. "We can go there. If we get off and the TGI Fridays is there, we're home-free. If not, we'd better buy kimonos and start learning how to make kimchi."

The conference began the next day, and I'm telling you, the worship time was a supernatural experience. People from different tribes and tongues all worshipping together took my breath away. It was a powerful sight to look over the crowd and see all the colors of skin and clothing, and to hear the different languages as we sang songs together that were popular worldwide. It truly was a cross-section of the world worshiping together. It was a small taste of Heaven. Graham Kendrick, who won a Dove Award for writing "Shine, Jesus, Shine," was leading worship, along with Scott Wesley Brown, another popular Christian artist.

After my experience with the man in the prayer room earlier that week, I kept feeling a pull to go back there alone to see what the Lord

might have in store. The second I walked in, I was immediately surrounded by seven people. And, just as suddenly, they began praying for
me. It was quite overwhelming and humbling at the same time.

This one man whom I had never seen before and who obviously did
not know me said, "Oh, you are a son of joy! God has placed a heart like
John the apostle inside you. If you had been at the last supper, you would
have been the one to lay your head on His chest." My legs gave out, and I
fell on my knees to the floor. I knew right then I was fixing to get wiped
out both emotionally and spiritually.

A voice rose up from the group and started singing. This woman's
voice was soft and beautiful. Then she looked at me and said, "The Lord
has gifted you to write songs. I see thousands of children around you, and
you are leading them in songs of repentance and salvation. The Lord has
these songs to give to you, and I see Him writing on the tablet of your
heart . . . writing these songs out. You've come up behind Him, and you're
looking over His shoulder to see what He's writing," she continued.

I was mesmerized.

"But you can't see any of the words He's writing," she continued.
"He's dipping the pen into an inkwell and coming back to the tablet and
writing the words. And He's dipping and writing. And dipping and writing. The problem is," she stopped and looked deep into my eyes, piercing
all the way to my soul, "there is no ink in the inkwell He's dipping into!
The inkwell is your heart, and the ink is His Word. There is no Word in
your heart for Him to draw from to reveal the songs He is writing for
you."

All the breath suddenly went out of me. She was right. I had not been
in the Word; I hadn't been praying. I had been stuck in this numb world
of limbo and had just been going through the motions, dry as a bone

doing what I knew to do. I had gone to one church for three years only because it had allowed me to play music and direct a youth choir. I had been attending New Song for a few months, but still, at this moment, the two words that most accurately described me spiritually were *dry* and *apathetic*. This woman could see that in me as the Lord revealed it to her.

As I sobbed and felt these prayer warriors closing in around me and interceding for me, Romans 8:26 kept rolling through my mind. I truly was at that point where I couldn't pray. I no longer knew what to say. But the verse kept repeating: "And the Holy Spirit helps us in our distress. For we don't even know what we should pray for, nor how we should pray. But the Holy Spirit prays for us with groanings that cannot be expressed in words."

Then, the breaking point came.

On my knees, with people all around praying for me, I heard the whisper of a woman. In the buzz of six people praying, she bent down and got right in my ear so that only I could hear her. "The enemy has sought to destroy you from your birth. I see forms of physical abuse and sexual abuse. But at one point in your life, the Lord said, *You won't touch him anymore.* And it all stopped. The Lord wants to tell you something today . . . you are not damaged goods."

I was stunned. Only Dr. Abney knew I felt like that. Only he knew that I felt worthless at times . . . like damaged goods. I had not ever told anyone else. So when this sweet woman shared those prophetic words with me, I knew the Lord had revealed that to her and that the movement of the Holy Spirit was real. In fact, it was then that I realized the reason I was in Korea, and it was not to lead worship. I was in Korea, at The Torch Center with 5,000 people from all around the world, so that in this one moment God could speak to me alone again.

Once I got home and began to process all that was spoken to me, I recalled the powerful, healing words the woman said. I remembered hearing the story of my birth, that I weighed eleven pounds, I was a month overdue, and both my mom and I almost died during the process. Then I remembered that April 1976 was the last time my daddy whipped me. April 1976 was also the last time my Great Uncle George molested me. Not long after that, he died. And I realized that it all stopped in 1976, the year our country was celebrating its freedom.

The year He set me free as well.

CHAPTER 10

REMIND ME, DEAR LORD

Feeling that freedom after I returned from Korea, I began to do those things I had not done in a long, long time. I jumped into the Word with an eagerness that had been missing for several years, and I spent the first part of my mornings in sweet and intimate conversations with the Lord.

By the end of May 1995, I was travelling to the First Baptist Church of Chatsworth, Georgia, for my first event since I came back to the States. I could feel the Lord prompting me to pray for that event and, to be perfectly honest, it was the first time I had done that before an event in a while. As I drove along on that Sunday afternoon, my prayer was not just for that night's event but for the people coming and for Him to do great things.

After I prayed, the Lord gave me an idea to do a section of the concert with songs I had sung as a little boy at my grandparent's house in Brazil, Mississippi. This was about a year before I started writing the VBS music, so the crowd that night was made up mostly of adults. I thought I'd break the ice by doing a little boogie woogie and played "Cotton Fields" to loosen them up.

My grandmother loved an old southern gospel song titled "Remind Me, Dear Lord," and that's the song I played right after "Cotton Fields." It's one of those songs from my childhood that made an indelible mark on my heart because it is a connection to my family heritage. I can remember watching my grandmother's face light up as she sang that song. She understood what those lyrics meant. "Roll back the curtain of memory now and then; show me where you brought me from and where I could have been. Remember I'm human and humans forget. So remind me, remind me, dear Lord." Later on, as I grew up, she loved to hear me sing that same song.

I used "Remind Me, Dear Lord" to lead us into a time of worship, and by the end of that song people started coming to the altar to kneel and pray. I could sense by the reaction of the crowd that this did not typically happen. I remember a lady approaching the pastor with a Bible in her hands. She opened it to a specific passage and shared it with him, after which he nodded and walked up to the pulpit. He grabbed a bottle of anointing oil, then motioned for me to stop playing so he could address the congregation.

"My sister here has come forward and told me she got a bad report of cancer from her doctor this week," he began. "She showed me the passage in Mark where the elders prayed for the sick and anointed them with oil . . . and they were healed. And she's asked me and the elders to do this for her tonight. I don't know where you stand in your belief in this," he continued, "so if this upsets you, I'm going to ask you to leave, because I don't want there to be any doubt or unbelief in this room when we pray for her."

Everyone stayed.

The men anointed this woman and prayed for her, and it was a moment when you could truly sense the Holy Spirit enveloping the whole room, and the presence of the Lord was thick. It was tender and powerful at the same time.

At the end of the service, the woman came up to me and said, "I have been a member of this church all my life. When I was a little girl, I was diagnosed with cancer, and the people of this church prayed fervently for me, and the Lord healed me. The Sunday after I had gotten a clean report from the doctor, I came here, and a man stood on the platform in almost the exact spot as you did tonight and he sang, 'Remind Me, Dear Lord.' Since that day there have been many times when I desperately needed to hear that song and couldn't find it. Well, this week I went back to the doctor and he told me my cancer had returned. Jeff, I came here tonight and you stood on that same stage and sang the very song I have wanted to hear since I was eight years old, the last time I was diagnosed with cancer."

I was overcome with the feeling that God ordained that night in a way I never would have experienced had I not been obedient. I began hashing out thoughts in my mind that had I not been so broken in Korea, had I not been prayed for and prophesied over, had God not revealed my empty inkwell to a woman I will never ever know. . . .

Had all that not happened, I may not have been compelled to begin pressing into the Lord and seeking time with Him. Because in that intimate time with Him, I learned how to trust Him again, and how to follow His leading, so that He could make this night possible. Obedience comes at a price, but so does disobedience. I had paid the price for the latter too many times.

This night in Georgia affirmed what I already knew: Claiming His calling in your life and trying to go through the motions with an empty inkwell produces nothing.

I could barely get to the car without breaking down. I was weeping and felt so convicted. The Lord taught me a beautiful lesson that night. *I've created you to be obedient to Me and follow Me. See what I can do if you just make a little effort? Don't ever think there isn't a reason or a direction. There is always a beautiful surprise awaiting you when you just listen and obey without question.*

Thank you for reminding me, dear Lord.

CHAPTER 11

MR. DAIGNEAULT'S OPUS

"We are your symphony, Mr. Holland. We are the melodies and the notes of your opus. We are the music of your life."

—Governor Gertrude Lang,
in the final scene of *Mr. Holland's Opus*

*M*R. *HOLLAND'S OPUS* IS THE STORY OF GLENN HOLLAND, WHO, AT AGE thirty, leaves the exhausting life of a professional musician to spend more time at home with his wife, and to compose what he is sure will be the orchestral piece—or "opus"—that will vault him to fame and riches. In the meantime, to make ends meet, he takes a teaching position at the local high school that he is sure will only be a temporary "gig."

Instead, he spends the next thirty years teaching music at John F. Kennedy High School in Portland, Oregon, and, in the end, never realizes his dream of becoming famous. At the close of his long career, having unwittingly inspired many of his students, he labels his life a failure. When the music program is erased by budget cuts, this defeated music teacher retires, packs up, and walks out of his classroom for the last time.

In a touching tribute in the final scene, Governor Gertrude Lang—who as a student twenty years before was musically challenged and struggled mightily with confidence before Mr. Holland intervened—is asked to return to her alma mater to pay homage to her mentor in front of a packed school auditorium. Governor Lang speaks of the profound influence her teacher had on her life, and her warm words ease his broken heart. Then, the curtains open and the stage is filled with three decades' worth of students whose lives had likewise been touched by Holland. In as grand a moment of esteem and affirmation as one could imagine, this band of former students plays the premiere rendition of *The American Symphony*, or, more accurately, *Mr. Holland's Opus*, the piece he had worked on for years but had never published.

On a cold January night in 1996, I walked out of a movie theater in Nashville, having just watched this wonderful movie, and made a promise to drive four-and-a-half hours to Grenada, Mississippi, to say "thank you" to David Daigneault, the man who, in great measure, was my Mr. Holland.

Today Dr. David Daigneault is the Superintendent of Schools in Grenada. For almost three decades, though, he was the band director at Grenada High School, where an average band program of 150 kids in 1980 grew to more than 800 by the year 2000 and became one of the most decorated high school marching bands in the country.

The Charger Marching Band has enjoyed a certain prestige within band circles all over the country, thanks to the dedicated leadership of Dr. Daigneault. Since he arrived in Grenada, his bands have accrued some sixty Grand Championships as well as Best in Class awards in eight different states. In 1995 and 2001, Grenada was the featured NBC band at the Macy's Thanksgiving Day Parade. In 1998 it marched in the Tournament of Roses Parade in Pasadena, California.

For its efforts, the Grenada Band was named the 1997 National High School Band of the Year, and Dr. Daigneault was designated as the National High School Band Director of the Year by the NHSBD Hall of Fame.

While all that is impressive, the real reason I was determined to drive four hours to Grenada, Mississippi, had little to do with my appreciation for his success there. But it had everything to do with a twelve-year-old kid who—like Governor Gertrude Lang—also struggled mightily with self-confidence and searched for who he was. In the midst of that search, a twenty-two-year-old band director cared enough to encourage and inspire him.

> *"There's a lot more to music than notes on a page. . . . It's about heart. It's about feelings and moving people . . ."*
> —Glenn Holland, *Mr. Holland's Opus*

Mr. Daigneault arrived at Pillow Academy, a private college preparatory school in Greenwood, Mississippi, in 1975. He had grown up in New Orleans and had a thick Louisiana drawl and an infectious energy and love for music, especially jazz. After graduating from the University of Southern Mississippi, he had come to teach kids about improvisation to help them learn to express themselves and be creative as musicians. When I began attending Pillow Academy in the fall of 1976, I was an eleven-year-old kid who was super excited about joining the band program there. His kind of teaching took root in me, and I thrived.

Before Mr. Daigneault arrived, I had grown up, like most kids in the south, in a culture that valued sports above almost anything. In fact, most allegiances went "football, family, and faith". . . mostly in that order. There was little room for kids like me who had a passion for music. Sports didn't make sense to me, and, on top of that, kids made fun of me because I was overweight, wore glasses, and took piano lessons. When I told my mama that the other kids were teasing me with "Slaughter house is for pigs!" jeers, she just threw her shoulders back and replied, "You just tell them you're God's little pig!" That didn't exactly make me feel better.

But playing the piano and singing did. I had already learned to play piano by ear, but eventually I began taking lessons under Mrs. Martha Hudson until she moved, and then Mrs. Ann Walker taught me all the way through high school. God blessed me with a sense of pitch and understanding of how music and words and instruments blended together to make songs work. Mr. Daigneault must have recognized some of that in me. I was still in his sixth-grade beginner band when he invited me to join the jazz band, which was largely made up of accomplished high school students.

At the beginning of that year, Mr. Daigneault encouraged me to play the tuba. He said I had the perfect "embrasure," which I later learned to mean I had the right spacing between my teeth, and that was good enough for me. I was determined to be the best tuba player around, so I lugged that big instrument from school, onto the bus, and all the way home. When I got home that first day, Mama looked at me, then down at that huge tuba, and back at me.

"Was there not anything else in that band you could play?"

"Well," I smiled as convincingly as I could, "Mr. Daigneault said I'd be perfect for the tuba because I have the embrasure for this and I am perfectly suited for it."

"Well, I think it's because you're the only one strong enough to carry that thing around."

By the end of the year, though, I had spent a lot of hours with that tuba, and I hoped I would receive the Outstanding Beginner Band Award. This award meant as much to me as the Heisman Trophy does to college athletes, or as the Oscar does to Hollywood actors. There were several in that band who were certainly talented enough to win that award as well, so I sat there with my fingers crossed, staring at Mr. Daigneault while he explained his decision on who should receive it.

"For this award," he said, "there was one obvious choice. This guy is a jack of all trades," he continued. When he said this, I thought, *Ohmigosh, I'm halfway there. It's a guy.*

"He can play anything he puts his hands on," Mr. Daigneault continued. "So, it is my pleasure tonight to announce this year's Outstanding Beginning Band Member Award goes to . . . Jeff Slaughter."

As he handed the award to me, Mr. Daigneault smiled. "Congratulations buddy . . . I'm so proud of you." I will never forget how I felt at that moment. I still have that trophy stowed away in a closet. Sometimes, when I do my spring cleaning, I take it out and remember the feeling I had that night. And how different my life is today because someone believed in me.

When we're young, how we feel about ourselves can be so skewed by the perceived value placed on us by our peers. We don't always see how others, such as influential adults, look at us. I never had a clue that someone would see me like Mr. Daigneault did. But what he saw in me and the value he put on my musical gifts changed my life.

He spoke life into my dreams. And that's what I wanted him to know when I went to see him in Grenada.

When I walked into his band room and saw him standing there with several students, it was as if I were back at Pillow Academy again. The smile, hair, and thick mustache were the same. So was that Louisiana drawl. Nothing really had changed much in the way Mr. Daigneault looked, nor in the fact that all the kids around him at Grenada obviously loved him, just like we did at Pillow.

"Not much has changed," I said, as I walked up to him. He looked up from his students and smiled.

"Jeff Slaughter!"

After a quick embrace, Mr. Daigneault introduced me to his students before we left to catch up over a cup of coffee. "Students, I want to tell you a story about this guy. When he was eleven years old, he was already a proficient musician, and as a sixth grader, he was in my first high school jazz band. I didn't know how good he was at playing the piano until one day we're all just kind of hanging around before class, and there were kids playing a few bars on their instruments, just being creative, and someone said, 'Let's hear Jeff play.' So I look at Jeff, and he looks up at me and asks if he could do his on piano. I'm telling you, kids. He had to sit on the very edge of the bench and stretch his toes out as far as he could just to reach the pedals to sustain a line. But, boy, when he started playing Christmas carols, it filled the room with the most beautiful music. I was blown away. That was twenty-six years ago, and I remember it like it was yesterday."

Later, as we sat down at a local coffee shop to talk, I tried my hardest to convey my appreciation to him for the role he played in my life.

"When I needed an adult to tell me there was something special in me and that I had something to offer, you were there," I told him. "All of the great things that have happened with my music are due in large part to you because of the encouragement you gave me and the influence you had over me at such a crucial point in my childhood."

"Look at you," he responded. "It's because of what you've done. It was obvious to me so long ago that you were given a great gift as a musician. But you were also given a great gift of caring for others and seeing something of value in them, even when you didn't feel that way about yourself. I knew that someday, if you could put those gifts together, music would be your vehicle to make a difference in the lives of other people. And that's what you've done."

Since that day, I've learned that ten of Mr. Daigneault's students have gone on to pursue music professionally, and scores of others have gone on to perform in churches or work in full-time music ministry and marching bands all over the country. One of his former band majors is an actress on Broadway.

Our society teaches us that when we look at people, we are supposed to judge them by their body of work, by portfolios that chronicle rewards and certificates and how high they have climbed corporate ladders. But for men like David Daigneault, who have certainly earned those accolades, those things don't matter so much. He can rest his head on a pillow every night knowing that he has reached people through music. Over a lifetime, he has used music as a vehicle to touch a lot of lives, and through humility he has embraced his calling and made thousands of kids believe in themselves.

I am who I am today in large part because of David Daigneault. My life is but one part of his opus, and along with all those other kids who have walked into his band room since 1975, we are the music of his life.

There is another poignant scene in *Mr. Holland's Opus* that comes to my mind. When the talented Rowena Morgan stood before her teacher at the bus stop just before leaving to chase her dream of singing on Broadway, she told Mr. Holland, "You love music, and you made the kids love it with you."

I can't think of a better way to say "thank you" than that. For David Daigneault did the same for me.

CHAPTER 12

PLAY SOME CON-WAAAYYY!

W HEN YOU'RE TWENTY-NINE YEARS OLD AND YOU WRITE A NUMBER-one song for a group like Point of Grace, you begin to get the idea you've got the whole Nashville music industry figured out. That's where I was in February 1994, when news broke of the ascension of "One More Broken Heart" to the top of the charts.

Since 1989, I'd had songs recorded by The Imperials, Steve Green, Truth, and Al Denson, but none of them had gone to radio. When I received the news about "One More Broken Heart," I figured I'd be hanging "No. 1" plaques on my wall for years to come. But two years later, when I walked into a smoke-filled VFW club to play a gig, I found out I didn't have anything figured out, except that I had a lot to figure out.

The Nashville music machine can be quite difficult to master. It's easy to get lost in thinking that if you have certain things in place, you should be able to make it. But I never seemed to "fit the mold" for what they were looking for, and that made it challenging. Lots of my friends were getting record deals and climbing the charts, and while I was super excited for them, I felt like I was falling behind. Up until then, I had been very confident something was going to happen, but now I was wondering if I was just spinning my wheels and simply needed to give up and go home.

I desperately wanted to make a living writing and playing music—it's all I'd ever wanted—so I prayed, "Lord, I want to do this, but help me bypass the whole machine of it all. Show me how to establish a new model that goes against the grain of what the industry says you have to do."

In August 1996 I got a call from a guy named Eric, who taught guitar at Shuff's Music Store in Franklin, Tennessee, where I had been teaching piano lessons since college. Eric called to invite me to sit in on keyboards with a band he was playing with.

Now the road that led me to Shuff's Music Store wasn't very long, but it was "scenic" to say the least. During a summer break from college in 1986, I started working with a few friends from Belmont, including Trisha Yearwood, at the Country Music Hall of Fame. I played piano for Trisha's voice lessons, and knew she had gotten hired as a tour guide there. She told me the CMHF was hiring, so I went down and was hired on the spot to work in the gift shop. Now I love and respect country music and the Country Music Hall of Fame, but due to my lack of knowledge of the history of it, I probably was not the most well suited person to work there. To compound the pressure, my first week on the job coincided with Fan Fare, and I had just finished training on the register. When you worked in the gift shop, you got a fifteen-minute break in the morning and another in the afternoon, with thirty minutes for lunch. That gave you just enough time to go across the street to Barbara Mandrell Country and grab a hot dog. Every day I had to wear khaki pants, a white, long-sleeved, button-down shirt, and a tie that had "Country Music Hall of Fame" written on it about 300 times. During that week of Fan Fare, some 55,000 adoring country music fans invaded Nashville, and I know every single one of them came through that gift shop.

On my first day, I was delighted to have music playing over the sound system while I was working, until I realized it was a loop of ten songs that played all day, every day. By my second week I went to the manager to see if there was another loop of songs we could play instead. "What music?" she asked. Apparently, once you worked there a while, you didn't even notice it anymore.

By my third day there, I could barely hear the music over the noise of the screams that emanated from the Elvis Presley theater, where people could go in and watch a short film of the King's life. It amazed me to see the number of people, men and women both, who walked out of the theater in tears and had to be held up by someone because of their grief.

It wasn't uncommon for the media to set up cameras and micro-phones to interview some of the country music stars who would come to visit with fans. One morning, I heard a guy's voice coming from the museum where all the glass cases containing memorabilia of various music stars were housed. I figured there was a television crew or radio personality there setting up to do an interview. When I stepped out of the gift shop to check things out, I saw this guy holding a small microphone and one of those hand-held, rectangular recorders from the 1970s, the kind where you have to press down the "play" and "record" buttons at the same time.

He was standing there in complete awe of his surroundings and speak-ing into the microphone. "Mother, I am standing in the hallowed halls of the Country Music Hall of Fame!" Then he saw me. Before I could even blink he was right in front of me telling his mother, "Ooohhh, here's a young man that works right here." I couldn't help but smile at the sheer joy he was experiencing. You'd have thought I was George Strait. "Son, has it been a liiiife-long dream of yours to work in this fine establishment?" As he stuck that mic in my face to record my answer for all posterity, I had a mental battle between whether I should tell him the truth, or make his day.

Obviously I had to make his day. "Bro, you don't even know. This truly is my dream come true. You want me to tell you who all has been in here just this week?"

He started jumping up and down and screaming into the microphone. Then he caught me off guard. "Now, who is your most favorite country singer?" Uh-oh. Hadn't planned on that. Not knowing what to say, I cleverly responded, "Who's yours?"

"Patsy Cline, of course."

"Ohmigosh, I love Patsy Cline, too." And I wasn't lying.

"Ooooh, Mother . . . he loves Patsy Cline just like we doooo." This sent him over the edge, and I figured that if I said much more, we might have to call the EMS, so I politely told him I needed to get back to work.

I never got to meet "Mother," but I'll bet that cassette tape is in a glass case of its own in her house.

RON SHUFF WAS THE OWNER OF THE MUSIC STORE, AND HE AND I MET AT church one Sunday during the summer of 1986. We had a strong connection immediately, and by the time our first conversation ended, he had offered me a job. The next day I went and turned in my neck tie to the CMHF, grabbed one more hot dog for the road, and headed south to Shuff's. At first I sold pianos before eventually moving into a position of solely teaching lessons, and I stayed there until 2002.

Ron would constantly get calls looking for someone to play at events. For most of them, they just wanted a pianist, so he farmed a lot of those requests out to me. On one of those occasions, a nursing home called and wanted entertainment for a special dinner banquet for the residents and their families. I was told I would simply provide the background music for dinner, and once they finished eating, I was free to go. While I was playing the last song before heading out the door, a man who worked for the nursing home walked up to the piano and looked at me. "We're ready for you to start the program now."

My eyes bugged. "Program?"

"Yes."

My ears started getting hot. "Ummmm. . . how long a program were you expecting?"

"Oh, I don't know. About an hour, I guess."

I just looked at him with a blank stare and thought, *Lord, Jesus, what am I gonna do?*

Suddenly, all those Sunday afternoons playing for my grandparents in Brazil, Mississippi, and weekends with the *Reader's Digest Family Songbook* at the Greenwood Country Club culminated in a fly-by-the-seat-of-my-pants program that, thankfully, became an instant hit. By the end, the residents were asking me when I could come back. And, to be honest, when the shock wore off from having to come up with something so off-the-cuff, I realized I had as much fun doing it as they had watching it.

I hadn't been working for Ron for very long when he got a call from a place called The Goose Creek Inn near Franklin that was hosting a Christmas party for a local business. At that point, I didn't even own a keyboard yet, so Ron sent me along with one of those party organs complete with bass pedals and preset drum beats.

In the reception hall, I watched women with big hair and even bigger shoulder pads mingle with men who were sporting parachute pants, flipped-up collars, and mullets.

During dinner, I played soft background music, which is what I had been hired to do. Just when I thought everything was winding down, a man walked up to me and yelled, "We wanna dance!"

I looked at the organ in front of me and thought, *You need a band, brotha. Ain't no way you gettin' dance music outta this.*

"Well, can't you play some disco on this thing?" the guy went on. And I thought, *Somebody's gonna be working hard for the money tonight, and it ain't gonna be Donna Summer.* Every time I think about that night, I still throw up in my mouth a little.

ELEVEN YEARS PASSED BY, AND I WAS THREE YEARS REMOVED FROM MY number-one hit with Point of Grace, when Eric called me and asked if I wanted to do that gig with him and his band. He gave me the address and told me when to meet him there for the sound check.

"We're mainly going to play some cover tunes, maybe a few originals. Easy money," he told me. Sounded good to me. I was leaving for a trip to Florida with some friends in a few days, and this extra money would help me have an even better time there.

So, on the appointed night, I drove up, took one look at the building, and thought, *This can't be it.* I looked down on the piece of paper with the address on it, matched it to the number on the building, and, sure enough, I was about to play a gig at a VFW club in one of the shadiest parts of town.

When I opened the door, a thick cloud of cigarette smoke came billowing out. I noticed about fifteen to twenty people milling about, chain smoking and guzzling beer. I'm sure about 80 percent of them didn't have teeth, and it seemed to have been a while since many of them had bathed.

Oh, did I forget to mention this was a two-night gig?

Not long into our first set on "opening night," the customers started raising their long-necks over their heads, yelling, "Play some Con-Waaayyy! Play some Con-Waaayyy!" all the while trying to keep the cigarettes from leaping off their lips onto the nasty floor. Not sure that would have mattered, because I'm certain they'd have just picked them up and resumed smoking.

Trevor Freeborn, the lead singer in the band, started looking around nervously at each person in the band. "Who knows some Conway Twitty songs?"

"Well," said Eric, offering information I didn't want to particularly share at that moment, "Jeff toured with Conway, and he knows all his songs." I looked at him in horror. My worst nightmare on a stage was about to take place.

Trevor looked at me with relief, as if to say, *Well, come on*, and I slowly ambled up to the mic with fear and trembling. The whole slow walk to "center stage," I was thinking, *Lord, I've hit rock bottom. I've been here in Nashville for eleven years, and tonight I am playing in a cover band, singing Conway Twitty songs in a VFW club for a bunch of folks with no teeth.*

Still not sure today if the money for the Florida trip was worth it.

But I'll tell you what was worth it. I was blessed to spend a lot of years working with a man that to this day I admire tremendously. Ron

Shuff became a dear friend and one of my biggest supporters. He was the only Kawai piano dealer in Middle Tennessee, and while I was in college I would teach lessons, then stay late so that I could practice on a Kawai.

Kawais are manufactured in Japan, and the company specializes in building the best concert pianos in the world. I always told Ron that one day I was going to buy one of those pianos. "Well, you know I'll make you the best deal you'll ever get on one," he'd smile.

In 2003, after my daddy died, the day I returned to Nashville following that long ordeal, I walked into my house and the phone started ringing. It was Ron. "Hey, buddy, I just wanted to make sure you were home and made it back all right. I've got a delivery I want to make to your house."

The next thing I knew, there were guys at my door hauling a baby grand piano into my house. It was a 75th Anniversary Kawai, one of very few that were built, and Ron made sure I got one.

True to his word, he gave me the absolute best deal I could have gotten. "You can pay me for this whenever you can," he winked. "But I want you to have it now."

Today, that same piano sits in my living room, where I have had the blessing of honoring such a wonderful man by using it to write songs that have shared the Gospel with some 46 million people around the world.

CHAPTER 13

DIVINE APPOINTMENTS

The Spirit of the Sovereign Lord is upon me, because the Lord
has appointed me to bring good news to the poor.
He has sent me to comfort the brokenhearted
and to announce that captives will be released
and prisoners will be freed.

—Isaiah 61:1

"As long as there is one more bridge to cross, an' one more mile to go . . . I'm go'n go!" Those were the words of an older black gentleman who taught the Bible to a bunch of high-risk teenage boys at a facility in Nashville known as the Spencer Youth Center.

While I was at Belmont University, a friend of mine named Clark wanted me to go with him and start teaching Sunday School there. I have always had a heart for elementary school kids, especially ones in an orphanage, so I figured this would be right up my alley. I had no idea that when I walked in the room, I'd be standing in front of a group of thirteen- to seventeen-year-old boys who had experienced more pain and tragedy than most of us could possibly imagine. These boys had committed crimes ranging from dealing drugs to manslaughter. They lived in prison-type cells, and most were already hardened by life and disappointment.

Thinking I would be leading worship for some sort of church or Sunday School–type service, I arrived with my keyboard, dressed in black pants, a sweater that embodied the style of the late 1980s—think Bill Cosby—and a pair of black tassel loafers. I was taken aback when armed guards militantly directed our "audience" in by single-file lines. They were completely quiet, save for the sounds of their feet shuffling across the floor. The smell inside was stale, the odor almost suffocating. There were no windows. There was no color. Everything about the atmosphere was stoic and cold, and it was reflected in the faces of these young men. For lack of a better phrase, their demeanor was void of life. The difference in our worlds provided a wide enough gap that making a connection was extremely difficult. Here we were, trying to tell them about the love of the Lord, and they just looked at us with cold, dead eyes.

The fact is, most of those young men had no reference to be able to understand God's love. Most believers have families, friends, and churches that represent a tangible demonstration of God's love in their lives. These boys, however, had none of that. And in a conversation I had with one particular young man, he said matter-of-factly, "If God loves me so much, I'd hate to see my life if He didn't."

At that moment, the Lord began to show me that the only way to have an impact on them was to come alongside that loving pastor, cross the bridge, walk the mile, and love them consistently and without condition. It wasn't easy. In fact, it was probably a near-impossible task. Still, the bridges were there, and there were many miles left to go.

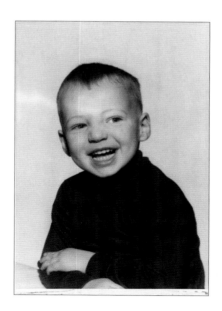

Cheesin' it up for the camera.
I'm about three or four years old.
(Credit: Olan Mills)

The Slaughter "glory days" in 1972. I think I needed to use the
bathroom. (Credit: Aunt Linda)

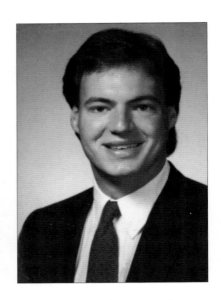

Got to switch from the tuba to the mellophone (or French horn) in high school. I was *so* proud of this uniform! (Credit: Lamb's Studio)

My "frat daddy" days at MS State. I had "KA" stitched on so many of my clothes that when I transferred to Belmont, my nickname was "Ka."

Bad hair days in 1985. I'd just gotten my one and only perm and was working up to a mullet. Mama is sportin' her County Market smock.

Dinner with legend Loretta Lynn in Gstaad, Switzerland, in 1989.

With Conway Twitty in Gstaad. I don't remember what he was saying, but it looks like someone was "gettin' tuned up!"

The 1993 Kenny Rogers Christmas
tour. I'm on the far left.

At Love Hall in Seoul, Korea, with my friend Tracy.

Leading worship in Naples, Italy, in 2004. (Credit: Betty McKay)

Praying with Rudolfo on the train out of Siena, Italy. (Credit: Linda Forrest)

Bess and Mallorie in my sister Vickie's "Star Quest" VBS Bible study room.

Minerva Hatcher Alexander. If I've ever met a saint in this world, it would be "Mimi"!

With my daddy Carl in 2001. Yes, I had bleached my hair blonde for reasons I can't remember. (Credit: Ruth Slaughter)

With the Durbin brothers, Wes, Jonathon, and Todd, in 2005.

Leading the song "It's All True" at kids camp. (Credit: Jeremy McCullough)

Gettin' crazy at camp.

Canaan Children's Home in Uganda.

From the "God Cares" video shoot at the C Lazy U Ranch in Granby, Colorado. (Credit: Kent Harville)

My friends, brotha's, and producers Spencer and Preston Dalton.

Vickie, Carla, and me with Mama at her seventy-second birthday party, three weeks before she passed on Christmas Day.

Every Sunday, Clark and I would go to meet the old pastor, and before we went to share scripture and music with the young men, he would lead a devotional time with us. On one particular Sunday, he was sharing from Isaiah 61 with the deepest of convictions. "As long as there is one more bridge to cross, one more mile to go . . . I'm go'n' go." Watching him minister to those boys each week, we believed every word of it.

"One more bridge to cross" was one of those phrases that just stuck with me, and I began to think about what the man was telling us. Throughout my life different people have told me, "Jeff, you are an 'Isaiah 61 man.'" It's a chapter filled with redemption, salvation, and justice. It's Isaiah trumpeting God's sovereignty to His people, honoring their faithfulness through tough times and rewarding them for their commitment to following Him. It's God trading "beauty for ashes, joy instead of mourning, praise instead of despair" (v. 3). Isaiah 61 has become a life chapter for me.

It is especially Isaiah 61:1 that speaks to me. "You are called to heal the brokenhearted and set the captives free." So between this scripture and the theme of an old black gentleman's life, I was compelled to write a song.

DWIGHT LILES IS A WELL-KNOWN SONG WRITER IN NASHVILLE, HAVING written some of Christian music's most powerful songs. As a writer myself, I was blessed with a gift for making melodies, but at such a young age, my lyric writing still had way to go. Most established writers in Nashville would not even consider taking time to help a college-age student who had aspirations of writing songs. But Dwight somehow saw something in me and took me under his wing. He mentored me and taught me a lot about the craft of writing lyrics.

I had signed as an exclusive writer with StarSong Publishing in the spring of 1989. One day Dwight and I met there to write, and I shared my idea for the song, along with some of the stories I had heard from the boys at the Spencer Youth Center. All of a sudden the first line was written: "I see people merely existing; I see vacant eyes full of pain." From there, the song almost wrote itself. It was amazing how God honored that time. We literally wrote it in one day. There were no tweaks, nothing to change.

Dwight and I sat in that small writer's room and started shaping a melody and hashing out lyrics. It was like playing ping pong back and forth; he'd write a line, and I'd write a line. When we finished, we felt like we had a song that would stir people's hearts. The chorus goes like this:

> *As long as there's one more broken heart*
> *One more crying soul, I'll go*
> *And I will love them, Jesus*
> *As long as there's one more needing you*
> *One more I can show your love*
> *As long as there's one more broken heart*

We pitched that song to several artists, but it wasn't until 1992 that we finally got someone to record it. In January of that year I took a position as a keyboardist on the worship team at Brentwood Baptist Church just south of Nashville. Once there, I quickly became friends with Rob and Cindy Sterling, who had written several youth musicals and were well established in the Nashville Christian music community. One Sunday morning after a service, Rob came up to me on stage, and during the course of our conversation, he said, "I'm producing a new girls' group called 'Say So.' Do you have anything you want to pitch?"

Immediately, I thought of mine and Dwight's song. When I told Rob about it, he said, "Sing it to me." So I sang the chorus.

"Get me a demo as soon as you can. I think that's really strong."

"Say So" was a group of four young ladies from Ouachita University in Arkansas who had recently been signed by Word Entertainment and were about to record their first album. Our song was the first one they put on hold for their project. During the process of recording in 1993, the girls changed their name, and after "I'll Be Believing" became a hit, the second single off Point of Grace's first album was our song, "One More Broken Heart." Some four years after it was written, "One More Broken Heart" was on its way to becoming the second hit for Point of Grace.

In December 1993 I had just finished touring with Kenny Rogers. Two months later "One More Broken Heart" went Number 1 on Christian charts. It had been five years since I worked with those kids at Spencer Youth Center, but I got to go back in 1994 and tell them I had written a song about them. "You guys really wrote this song, not me or my friend Dwight," I said to them. "It's based on your stories, and now people all over the country are being touched by your lives. The Lord has blessed it and has taken it to the Number 1 spot on the charts."

As I sang the song for them, I wasn't expecting a huge response from boys so broken and abused. To be sure, though, it did feel as if something shifted in the air that day, and that space so void of life began to be filled some by hope. The windowless room seemed to brighten, if only just a little bit.

My first VBS, "The Wild and Wonderful Good News Stampede," came out in 1997, and that fall, following the VBS "season," I was at the First Baptist Church in Ripley, Mississippi, leading worship one Sunday morning. During the course of the worship time, I sang "One More Broken Heart" and shared the story behind it. I spoke of the young men who lived at Spencer Youth Center and how they doubted the love of Christ because of the blows life had dealt them and the things they had done that resulted in their being sent there. I told them about this pastor who was steadfast in sharing Christ with those young men over the years. I couldn't help but smile as I told the crowd how determined he was to cross every bridge and walk every mile set before him in his life to share God's love.

Following the service, a young man in his late twenties approached me. Even with a shirt and tie, he looked disheveled and worn. Life had obviously been challenging, and it looked like he was beaten down. The rough years of childhood and struggles of adult life had certainly taken their toll on him. He just looked . . . tired.

"I just moved here, and I'm kinda starting over," he told me after introducing himself. I noticed how awkward he was. "I came here looking for work, and I haven't had much luck. But I woke up this morning feeling like I needed to go to church. To be honest, I really didn't want to go. I haven't been to church since I got to Ripley. It's been a while since I've been to church anywhere. I wasn't sure which one to go to. Something told me I needed to come to this one."

I nodded, wondering the whole time why he was sharing this with me. That is, until he said, "I walked in and you started talking about where I came from. I was at the Spencer Youth Center. I've done many things that I'm not proud of, and it's gotten me in a lot of trouble over the years. I thought there was no hope for me. Until today. Sometimes you get to the point where you think nobody cares. That you don't matter."

My voice choked when I said, "The Lord knew you needed to be encouraged today. Look how much you matter to Him. He was drawing you here so we could meet and both be encouraged. He knows your name, bro, and He loves you." The Divine Appointment was undeniable. "What are the chances that you would come here today and I would be here too? There is no other way to explain it than it was God setting this whole thing up."

As he wept, I prayed for him, and gave him a hug.

It was the only time I ever saw him. But I believe God orchestrates Divine appointments to show people how much He cares, no matter what they've done in life. And He uses the songs of people from completely different backgrounds and the determination of men who see one more bridge to cross, one more mile to go, as they boldly proclaim, "I'm go'n' go."

CHAPTER 14

FREEDOM

In 1998 a fifty-two-year-old man received a heart from a fourteen-year-old girl, and it was one of the "fullest" hearts an organ recipient ever received. I know this because I knew that fourteen-year-old girl.

Mallorie Kate Thomason was bright and funny and compassionate and cherished every moment with her family. She was the life of the party, loved to laugh, and forever looked for the "underdog" kid who needed a friend. She was part tomboy, part "girlie"—which made her a little boy crazy—and she loved to do the Sunday crossword puzzle with her granddaddy. She was barely a teenager and possessed the typical silliness of a girl just a few months out of middle school, but she also had the focus and diligence of a young adult.

And, oh, how she loved to worship. She recognized the power of worship and prayer, and not long before her tragic death made the statement that she couldn't wait until the people of her church would "raise their hands in worship."

I know all this about Mallorie Kate Thomason because I am her uncle, and the day of her funeral more than 1,000 people worshiped like never before inside North Greenwood Baptist Church.

IT WAS LATE AUGUST 1998, AND I WAS BEGINNING TO FEEL THE EFFECTS of a season of doing numerous Vacation Bible School events, kids camps, and concerts. I had just returned to Nashville from doing the Summer Youth Celebration camp in British Columbia with my friend, Tom Blackaby. His father, Henry, developed all those great Experiencing God studies. Having been home from Canada just a couple of days, I was anxious to get on the road for the long drive to my parents' home in Carrollton, just a few miles from where I grew up in Greenwood.

I ran into Dave Hunt, a talented worship leader who's been nominated for a Dove Award and has a cut on Casting Crowns' Lifesong project, in the parking lot of the LifeWay building in Nashville as I was on my way to Mississippi for the Labor Day weekend.

In 1998 Dave was a worship leader for Centrifuge Student Camps and had produced a CD project titled *Freedom*. When Dave saw me walking out to my car, he asked me how my summer had been. He was carrying a box of those *Freedom* CDs and handed me one. I had an armful of stuff I needed to take with me to Carrollton, so I tossed it all, including the CD, into the backseat of my new Pathfinder, which I couldn't wait for my family to see, especially Mallorie and her sister, Bess.

There was something about those two girls that I loved so much. They were close not only because they were sisters, but also because they were best friends. Mallorie was eighteen months older than Bess, and even though she had just started high school, they still shared a room, clothes, and talks about boys. Maybe they were so close because that's the way our family is. They had an older brother, Jay, who was in his second year of college then, and a younger brother, Sumner, who was in the second grade, so being close in age drew Mallorie and Bess together more than anything. I'm sure they were also close because they had both had to endure several painful surgeries on their legs from a form of Ricketts that had made their legs bow. Between the numerous operations and the braces strapped to their legs to straighten them, they had finally gotten to the point where they were walking a lot better. Maybe that's why they possessed such compassion for the underdog.

While Bess was creatively gifted—today she's a great teacher and a brilliant artist—Mallorie was very athletic, despite the problems with her legs. Ricketts may have stunted her growth but not her spirit. I said earlier how she was part tomboy, but still had a lot of "girly" in her. She had brown hair and these piercing green eyes. She was beautiful. And without even trying, she could make you roll on the floor with laughter. I remember one year she got training bras for Christmas, and she was so embarrassed when she opened the box in front of everybody that she threw them across the living room and ran out.

But if there was one thing that defined Mallorie for who she really was, it was her affinity for writing letters. She was passionate about writing words of encouragement to many, many people. She loved that I was a worship leader and was so proud of the work I was doing with VBS. My CD *Sun on My Face* hadn't been released for very long before she was listening to it constantly. She was thrilled that I was traveling to so many places, doing concerts, and leading worship. I know I got a letter from her at least once a month.

One of the greatest moments of my life was when I got to lead worship for the first time at at my home church during its Vacation Bible School. StarQuest was my second VBS with LifeWay and followed 1997's "The Wild and Wonderful Good News Stampede." My sister Vickie, along with her daughters Mallorie and Bess, helped me that week, and together we had an incredible time.

Vickie taught the fourth- through sixth-grade bible study, and Bess volunteered to decorate her room. Let me just say that she absolutely knocked it "out of this world" with stars and galaxies, and when Vickie's students walked into that room, they completely forgot that they were in a Sunday School room. Some of those kids have come back as adults to work VBS at North Greenwood, and they still talk to Bess and Vickie about the memories they have of that room.

That one week was a fulfillment of the dream I had back in the days of walking from school to church for piano lessons and my mom hosting and preparing the Wednesday night family meals. I knew back then that I wanted to do something musically that would get the whole church family involved, but I had no idea what that would look like.

When I pulled up in front of J. Z. George High School to pick up Mallorie and Bess, the looks on their faces were priceless. Their eyes bugged out when they saw my new Pathfinder, and they jumped in. Mallorie peered around the inside in amazement and then looked at me with this genuine, happy expression. "This is awesome!"

"Let's go cruise the big city and get some ice cream," I smiled. You should know the "big city" of Carrollton is exactly one square mile, and, as of the 2000 census, exactly 408 people lived inside the city limits.

Vickie and her family lived in a cottage on the property right behind my parents' house. Vickie has muscular dystrophy, so it made it easier for her to have Mama and Daddy right there. Their homes sit way out on Barefoot Road, and, true to "country livin,'" their nearest neighbors were about a quarter of a mile down the road.

Living in the country provides a lot of pleasures that people in the suburbs and the cities never experience. Morning is as simple an indulgence as there is. I can't speak for anyone else, but on Barefoot Road, as the sun rises, the coffee brews, and the humming bird feeders come alive, there isn't a better spot in the world to watch it all unfold than sitting in the sun room next to the back porch of my parents' home.

While Daddy was out dove hunting with my sister Carla's husband Tony that morning, I went to have a cup of coffee with Vickie in her kitchen. We were listening to *Sanctuary*, one of Twila Paris's best projects. We were so inspired that we began to sing along to one of our favorite hymns, "When the Roll Is Called Up Yonder," when Mallorie walked in and joined us. The three-part harmony that emanated from the kitchen on that September morning was beautiful.

As noon approached and Mama was preparing lunch, Vickie, her husband, Ken, and I were waiting for Carla to arrive. As we were talking, laughing, and generally catching up, Mallorie's friend Shelly Jo came riding up on a four-wheeler through the front yard and headed back to Vickie's house. Our family didn't have four-wheelers, but a lot of Mallorie's and Bess' friends did. Vickie didn't mind her girls riding with their friends, so long as they stayed in the pasture—never on the roads—and always wore helmets.

A few minutes later, we heard the four-wheeler fire up and saw it come flying around the front of the house. When it came into view, there was Shelly Jo driving, with Mallorie sitting on the back. The next thing we knew, they took off down the gravel road. I remember seeing Mallorie reach back to grab the rack behind the seat, sit up real high, and flip her shoulder-length hair back so that she could look straight up and soak in the sun and blue sky.

"Look at that," Vickie said. "I have told her never to ride a four-wheeler in the road, and she's not even wearing a helmet."

Get in your car and stop her, I heard a voice say in my head. The message was plain as day, and the impression was strong. Seconds later, it came again: *Get in your car and stop her*. I wondered if I was just having strange thoughts, or if the Lord was really trying to tell me something.

Then I heard, *That will be the last time you see her like that.*

> *The Lord is close to the brokenhearted,*
> *And saves those who are crushed in spirit.*
>
> —Psalm 34:18

FIVE MINUTES LATER, THE PHONE RANG, AND WHEN IT DID MY HEART stopped. Somehow I knew what was coming. Bess answered. "What?! *What*?! Oh, no!!" Bess was in the kitchen and started yelling for Vickie in a state of panic. "Mom, Mallorie's been in a wreck!"

Ken, Bess, and I jumped into Ken's truck and headed down Barefoot Road to find Mallorie. I can't begin to describe the scene as we drove up to see the mangled four-wheeler lying sideways and a red sedan hovering near a ditch. On the right side of the road, Shelly Jo was motionless and unconscious. When I saw her, I thought she was dead. She was unresponsive, and her breathing was very shallow, but she was still alive. Two boys walked aimlessly close by, looking pale and not knowing what to do. They had been on four-wheelers, too, and were with the girls when the crash occurred.

On the left side of the road lay Mallorie. She was conscious, but had some severe injuries. By looking at the proximity of the four-wheeler to the red sedan, it was obvious Mallorie had flown off the four-wheeler at impact and crashed into the windshield of the car. Blood was coming out of her ear, and her lip was split down the middle, which revealed that several of her teeth had been knocked out. Her left leg had been ripped open and was gushing blood.

My first inclination was to stop the bleeding, but every time I touched her she screamed in pain. I had to distract her and get her talking. "How many fingers am I holding up?" I asked her.

"Two."

"When is your birthday?"

"December 2, 1983."

"What is today?"

"September 5."

In my mind, I was sizing up the situation and assessing the damage to her face to figure out how we were going to fix everything. They can sew up her lip, she can wear false teeth, get plastic surgery. Her leg will have to be sown up, but that'll heal just fine. Everything is going to be okay.

Suddenly, I became aware of the Mississippi heat. The air was so thick that I felt like I was breathing cotton. Mallorie was sweating, and the dust from the dirt road had settled on her like a ton of makeup. The dust was still ominously swirling around the wreckage. It had certainly played its part in this horrendous crash. The two boys explained that they were friends of the girls; each had been riding his own four-wheeler, and Shelly Jo had been driving behind them. She and Mallorie had passed the first boy and had turned around to wave and laugh at him. The boy in the front of the pack had pulled up when his hat flew off his head, and he had turned around to retrieve it.

Because of so much dust, the visibility on the road had been compromised. When the girls had approached a curve in the road, they were paying more attention to the boys behind them than the road, and that's when the red sedan, driven by another teenage boy, had come speeding toward them. The result was a horrible, head-on collision.

The accident had taken place just in front of a man's house. Mallorie had given him the phone number to contact us. By the time we arrived, he had run back to his house and put ice in a plastic bag, and he was now on his knees, gently dripping water over her mouth from a small hole he had cut in the bag.

I could hear a car approaching from behind and knew it was Vickie and Mama. As Vickie slowly got out of the car, it was obvious she was having a hard time processing the scene. She was moving slowly, not just because of her muscular dystrophy, but because she was in a state where reality and the hope that everything will be okay come together almost as if in a dream. Before she could shut the car door behind her, I ran up to her.

"How bad is it?" she asked, but I felt sure she already knew.

"It's really bad, Vickie, so brace yourself. She doesn't need to see us freak out."

She stood there frozen for a moment, fighting back all her natural, maternal emotions. She drew in a deep breath and set her eyes like flint, with a determination I had never seen in her face before. "Let's go," she said.

As she slowly walked over to Mallorie, I watched Vickie swallow hard while her daughter saw her and started frantically apologizing. "I'm so sorry Mama! I'm so sorry! I know I wasn't supposed to be on the road. I know I was supposed to wear a helmet. I'm so sorry! I'm so sorry!"

Vickie did something her condition would otherwise have prevented her from doing: She knelt down. A calm came over her, and she gently stroked Mallorie's hair. "It's okay baby. I love you. You're my first baby girl. I love you with all my heart. The ambulance is going to be here soon, and you're gonna be okay." There was a lot of fear, panic, and pain on Mallorie's face. But a mother's heart always knows what to do. "You know what?" Vickie continued in that soft, soothing voice. "Let's just sing." Then she looked at me with steely eyes and a firm jaw and said, "Start singing."

We struggled through a couple of songs we loved. There was "Sunrise," "Mountain Move," and "Lord, I Lift Your Name on High."

Mallorie loved the group Avalon, and one of her favorites by them was "Testify," so she sang the chorus as best she could: "For as long as I shall live, I will testify to love; I'll be a witness in the silences when words are not enough. With every breath I take, I'll give thanks to God above; for as long as I shall live, I will testify to love."

In my heart I could feel the Lord tugging at me, playing images through my mind of all the years I had been leading worship, all the times I had declared through songs the things I believed about Him. It was as if in doing so, He was asking me, *Do you believe today? Will you praise me from sunrise to sunset today? Do you believe that there is nothing you need that I can't provide today?*

The eyes of the Lord are on the righteous
And his ears are attentive to their cry.

—Psalm 34:15

When the ambulance arrived at the scene, I climbed into the back to help the paramedic steady the girls' gurneys, even though it was against the rules. Both girls were on backboards, with their heads taped down, but on this uneven, rocky road, every bump caused the boards to shift. The pain must have been terribly intense for them. The driver was flying, and it was all the other paramedic and I could do to hold them steady. Mallorie cried out several times before we finally made it to the paved road.

Once we got to the hospital, they took the girls into the emergency room for evaluation. As Mallorie lay on a steel table, doctors immediately started cutting off her clothes to begin the process of assessing all the physical damage. Nurses were firing off questions at me, asking me her name, age, and birthday. One of the nurses then asked me about any medications she might be taking. I knew she was taking something but didn't know the name, so I asked Mallorie. It was a typical medication that few people can pronounce, much less spell, and Mallorie did both.

I sighed a breath of relief. Her mind was still sharp. She was going to be okay.

The doctors asked me to leave the ER area, so I walked over to Mallorie and said, "I love you, hon. I'll see you real soon," and turned to walk out of the room. As I made my way to the door, little did I realize that those would be the last words she would hear me say . . . or that I would be the last person in my family to see her conscious.

Andy Perry, a paramedic who is a close friend of the family, was Mallorie's Sunday School teacher. He was able to go back to be with her for a while. When he walked back into the waiting area where our family was sitting, I looked at the expression on his face, and I knew it was bad. My daddy had arrived just before Andy had gone to check on Mallorie.

Daddy had gotten word about the accident while sitting in a cotton field bird hunting, and I was standing by him, explaining as much as I could. Moments later, Andy walked back toward us. By law, he wasn't allowed to discuss anything about Mallorie's condition with us, but his demeanor told me everything I needed to know. All he could say was that by the time he got back there, Mallorie didn't know who he was and that he thought her brain might be swelling.

The next thing we knew, Mallorie was being placed in a helicopter to be air-lifted to Le Bonheur Children's Hospital in Memphis. The doctor took Vickie and Ken, our friend Margaret, and me into a small conference room to tell us what was happening. As we stood there, trying to focus on what the doctor was saying, we were numb. We heard something about the damage to her head, her brain swelling, and the need to air-lift Mallorie to Memphis. Beyond that, it was a blur. After the doctor left, we stood there in silence, the four of us in that room, each feeling like we were all alone and stunned by the events of the day. All of a sudden, Vickie shivered.

"Did you feel that?" she asked. None of us felt anything.

"It was like something wrapped around me. Like a breeze whipped around me."

The drive to Memphis was about two hours. While I drove, I called a few family members on my cell phone and told them to spread the word while Daddy sat quietly, almost in a trance, wondering if things would have been different had he not gone bird hunting. He was sure he would have prevented Mallorie from getting on that four-wheeler, and he was mentally beating himself up for not being there. By the time we arrived at Le Bonheur Children's Hospital, our cousin Al was waiting for us. We were quickly ushered to a family waiting room, where the doctor there began to apprise us of the extent of Mallorie's injuries.

"Mallorie has suffered a subdural hematoma," he said.

"What does that mean?" my daddy asked, hoping it wasn't as bad as it sounded. "Is she going to be all right?"

"I'm sorry," the doctor replied, slowly and gently, as if somehow he could soften the blow. "But Mallorie's brain has swelled beyond the capacity her skull can hold. When that happens, it goes the only place it can . . . down the brain stem. As the swelling continues down the stem, it begins to crush all the centers of breathing and other major bodily functions."

This was not what we wanted to hear. The doctor had not yet shared the worst of the news, but we could both sense what was coming, and Daddy's breathing got heavy with panic. It was the kind of gasping for breath someone has when he's about to have a heart attack. "What are you trying to say, doctor? Just tell us. What are you saying?"

"Well, I'm saying Mallorie's brain is completely damaged. It's completely dead. And . . . she is not going to make it."

Daddy leaned back hard in his chair and wailed with a sound I'd never heard come out of him. I sat there stunned for a moment. Finally, he looked at me and said, "Call your mama."

"Daddy, I can't call and tell her this over the phone," I shot back.

"Call your mama!"

I walked off to find a private place to do this, but as I pulled her number up and was about to press send, I slid down the wall in agony until I was on the floor. *I can't do this! I can't do this!* I said over and over to myself. That's when I turned my head and saw Mama and Vickie walking toward me.

"What's going on?" Vickie asked anxiously. I got up, and we walked into the room where Daddy was sitting.

"We just met with the doctor." I was trying to keep my composure, and I was having visions of our own sweet childhood. Our family's life had been so safe and secure, but all of that was going to be gone after this one day. "Vickie, this is the hardest thing I've ever had to do, and I don't know how to tell you this." The whole time she was looking at me, and her eyes were saying: *Don't say it. Don't you say this to me!*

I took a deep breath. "Here's what he said. . . ."

Finally, she looked up with fire in her eyes. "I don't care what the doctor said. The Lord can heal her. The Lord can raise her up. It's not over! Don't you believe that? Don't you, Jeff? Can't you feel that?"

"Yes, I believe He can heal her."

As family and friends gathered late that afternoon, we were given a waiting room just for us. Once we all got inside, Vickie had already formulated a plan. "We are going to sing, and we are going to pray, and we are going to read the Word . . . and we are going to do it for as long as it takes." So, we sang and prayed and read all night long. Mallorie was battling for her life. We were going into battle with her, and we were going to do it like the children of Israel did in II Chronicles when Jehoshaphat appointed a choir to wear holy robes and march ahead of the troops as they went to battle. It was Jehoshaphat's resolve that the children of Israel would express their reliance on the Word of God and would do so by singing His praises before they entered into battle.

I remember going down the hall just to walk for a while and coming back to hear the beautiful harmonies drifting down the hallway as my family sang. There's something that happens when you are singing praise to the Lord, and God encompasses that praise. The sound becomes supernatural. I don't really know how to explain it except to say that it goes beyond human singing, as if angels are joining in as well.

Later that night, a nurse walked into the family waiting room. We had not seen her before, because she worked on the floor above us. She had a sweet smile and a soft voice, and when she poked her head in the room, we thought she was going to ask us to take it down a notch. "Is that ya'll singing in here?"

"Yes, it is," Vickie said. "Are we too loud?"

"No," she said, as a smile crossed her lips. "I just wanted to tell you that we could hear you all the way up on our floor. It sounds like angels going up and down the hall upstairs."

The doctor had given us the freedom to come and go in Mallorie's room to sit with her. In his compassion, he was simply giving us time to get used to the inevitable. I remember going back and noticing how radiant she was. There was a glow surrounding her. I prayed for her as I hovered over her, and put my face to her face, my hands in her hands. I did everything I had ever read in the Word that brought about a miracle.

My mother joined me a while later and was so overwhelmed with grief that she was almost in shock. At her breaking point, she was yelling at me, begging, "Tell her to rise up and walk. Tell her, Jeff! You can tell her!"

Through tears I said, "Mama, I've done everything I know to do."

Finally, at about four o'clock in the morning, the doctor came to let us know it was time. There had been no brain activity at all, and they needed to unplug her from the machines and let her die peacefully.

We went to say our final goodbyes, and Vickie wailed with a deep, primal, wounded sound. The sound of ultimate sorrow.

It wasn't until 11:00 that Sunday morning that we were able to leave Memphis and return to Carrollton, and during the long, silent car ride home, no one said a word. Once home, we would have to go through the painful business of planning Mallorie's funeral and burial. The only positive thing about the whole weekend was the fact that Mallorie had declared to her mother a few weeks before that when she got her driver's license, she was going to be an organ donor. So, Vickie signed all the necessary papers to allow the doctors to harvest her organs.

By the time we drove down Barefoot Road near the spot that claimed our Mallorie's life, we were pulling up to a house where a yard full of cars were parked, and dozens of people from our church were waiting for us.

"We can't live here anymore," my mama said. We all know our mamas' voices so well and what they sound like. In that moment, her voice was devoid of the joy, life, and emotion that set her apart from so many. Instead, her voice was flat and numb. "There are too many memories here. We have to move."

As we slowly got out of the car, our friends were there to love on us. For years, these people had shared life with us. We all grew up together, and were in church plays together; we did Wednesdays and weddings and VBS and children's choir together. They embraced us and were crying with us . . . the very picture of the body of Christ that Paul wrote about.

We hadn't been inside the house long before the telephone rang. It was the woman from the organ donor agency that had been with Vickie when she signed the release forms. "I just want to let you know that Mallorie's heart is about to be transplanted into a fifty-two-year-old man with three kids. I'll let you know how it turns out."

A few hours later, there was another call. This time the woman specifically asked to speak with Vickie. "I wanted to call again and let you know that the surgery was a complete success, and Mallorie's heart was a perfect match."

"I knew it would be," Vickie gently replied.

In all, ten of Mallorie's organs were transplanted, including her sparkling green eyes.

The next morning, as Mama and Daddy sat silently in the sun room drinking coffee, I grabbed a cup and walked it down to Vickie's. As I made my way back to her bedroom, I set the cup on the nightstand, and sat down beside her on the bed. She was lying on her back, staring at the ceiling, and tears were slowly rolling down the sides of her face.

"How are we going to keep living now?" she asked.

"I don't know."

"Today is the first day in fourteen years I have woken up without my baby being in the world."

I will bless the name of the Lord at all times;
His praise will always be on my lips.

—Psalm 34:1

WHEN IT CAME TIME TO TALK ABOUT MALLORIE'S SERVICE, VICKIE WAS adamant. "I want you to lead worship," she told me, "and I want you to do it the way you always do, with the drum machine and your motions. I want you to do it just like Mallorie would have wanted you to if she were here. She always said, 'I can't wait until the people of North Greenwood raise their hands in worship.'"

We went on to plan how the service would flow, including the music that would be playing when people came in. We figured between our church family and school friends and all the people Mallorie had touched, we would probably have a big crowd.

"When people start coming in, I'd give anything if we could play that CD Mallorie wanted to buy this past summer at Centrifuge," Vickie said, almost in passing. "That's all I heard from her when she got home from camp: 'Can we order this CD? Can we order this CD?' But I just never got around to it."

"Centrifuge CD?" I asked. Instantly, the previous Friday morning came to my mind, where I had met Dave Hunt in the LifeWay parking lot.

"Yeah, I think it's called *Freedom*," Vickie said. My heart stopped and tears began to pool in my eyes as the realization started to sink in as to how the Lord had ordered my steps and orchestrated that meeting just a few days before.

I walked out to my car and rummaged around the backseat. There it was. I retrieved the CD and staggered back in the door, and as soon as Vickie saw it in my hand, her eyes widened, and she weakly said, "Where did you get that?"

I could barely get the words out of my mouth. For a moment, they were stuck in my throat, and I wasn't sure if I could speak them through the tears and brokenness. "Before I left Friday, I bumped into the guy who recorded it, and he gave it to me. The Lord knew we were going to need it. He knew you'd want to play this tomorrow."

For a long time, neither one of us spoke another word. There was this blend of raw emotion—a deep sorrow, yet knowing in the middle of the pain that the Lord cares. He was reminding us as believers that He walks with us through the hardest moments of our lives, and takes care of even the smallest details. In sweetness and sadness, frustration and pain and beauty . . . in all of it, He knows.

In all of it, He cares.

On the day of the funeral, 1,200 people packed our church. All seats were full, including those in the choir loft, and people were lined up along all of the walls. As I walked up to the keyboard on the stage and prepared to lead worship "just as if Mallorie was there," I prayed for strength. As I stood at the microphone before that crowd, I didn't know how to start. The only thing that came to my mind was Psalm 34:1: "I will bless the name of the Lord at all times; His praise will always be on my lips." I remembered it from my childhood. With no other plan, I started there. Each time I said it into the microphone, it gave me strength. Three times I repeated that verse, and, finally, I was strong enough to do the hardest thing worship-wise that I had ever tried to do.

Then I looked at the throngs of people there. "What you're about to experience will probably be the most unconventional thing you've ever witnessed in a service like this. But I don't care. There are only three things that matter today: Honoring the memory of my niece, comforting my family, and worshipping the Lord with gladness on the saddest day of our lives. So here we go."

I hit the drum machine and started leading motions, and soon people were clapping and singing, and you could feel joy coming into this place. After a few songs like "Sunrise" and "Mountain Move," I decided the time was right to ask everybody to do what Mallorie had wanted them to when she was alive. "My niece always said she'd love to see the day when the people of this church raised their hands in worship," I confessed. "I'm going to ask you to do this today. No matter how you may feel about it. Let's all lift holy hands to our Daddy and ask Him to help us." Down in the front row, I saw this grandfatherly type slowly begin to raise both of his hands, with his head bowed down in worship. It was my daddy. Though his face was wracked with pain, he bowed his head in reverence anyway and worshipped from the depths of his heart.

For that forty-five-minute period of time, people inside that church worshipped freely in a way they had never worshipped before. It was exactly the type of service that Mallorie would have absolutely loved.

A couple of weeks later, Carla wrote to Vickie and described to her a vision she had about Mallorie after she died. "I saw the Lord come down on a white horse, and He rode up to Mallorie and gently said, 'It's time to go.' Mallorie smiled and said, 'Can I have a cloak of comfort to wrap around my mother before I go?' I saw the Lord hand her the cloak, and she walked over to wrap it around you. Then she turned back to the Lord and said, 'Okay, I'm ready.'"

The power of those words resonated with Vickie because she remembered very distinctly the moment in the waiting room when she had felt a "breeze" encircle her. She believed, as did I, that it was the cloak of comfort Mallorie placed around her that made her shiver. What made Carla's words so amazing was that she wasn't even in the room when it happened, and we had not said anything to her about it.

And so we moved on as a family, but there's always this gaping hole. There are Christmases where we decorate the tree, and someone finds the homemade ornament with a handwritten note, "To MeeMee, from Mallorie," and silently places it on the tree with quiet tears. We still laugh and tell stories, and life goes on . . . but it's never been the same. My daddy never picked up a gun again. He went the rest of his life thinking that he could have prevented Mallorie's death if he had just been there and not sitting in a cotton field on a dove shoot. After that event, he never had the desire to hunt again.

Then there are the group pictures where she was there, and the ones taken after she died. The looks in our eyes are so different in the later ones. Grief changes you. For me, there is something about learning how to let go. You don't ever quit loving, but you have to hold on loosely because there is a time appointed for everyone to be born and a time appointed for them to die. I hesitated that day before her accident when God told me to get in my car and stop her. I've often wondered what might have been had I listened. I don't hesitate any more when I feel Him telling me to do something.

HELEN KELLER ONCE SAID, "THE BEST AND MOST BEAUTIFUL THINGS IN the world cannot be seen or even touched—they must be felt with the heart." After Mallorie died, her heart was the first of ten of her organs that was transplanted. I thought that was fitting because she had such a heart for God and for people.

Vickie had tossed around the idea of starting a Bible study with some ladies in her church that would focus on the heart. She found out some pretty neat things about the heart, like if you were to stretch out in a straight line all the veins that run blood through the body and connect to the heart, that line would stretch all the way around the world.

But what caught her eye even more was when she discovered that science has proven that the human heart stores emotion. So when the Lord said that the heart was the temple of God, it makes sense that all your love and emotions and desire for the Lord are summed up in the saying that "she had such a heart for Jesus" or "we are to serve with all of our heart." The heart truly is the wellspring of life.

A year after Mallorie's funeral, a letter came in the mail from the man in Tennessee who had received her heart. Knowing her name was Mallorie

Kate, he called his heart his "Little Katie." "I want to thank you for your gift of life to me," his letter said. "I know I wouldn't be celebrating another birthday today without my 'Little Katie.' In your grief and sorrow you were willing to help someone else, and I am alive today because of that gift. "

A year later another letter arrived from the same man around Christmas. "I have some questions to ask you about Mallorie because I am a different man than I was two years ago. Did Mallorie write letters? I am an uneducated man who never would write letters because I have always been self-conscious about my spelling. But my heart—my 'Little Katie'—won't let me not write you. I'm fifty-four now, and I've never written letters in my life. But now I write them constantly. Did Mallorie love worshipping at church? I go to church and I raise my hands, and I never raised my hands before. My wife looks at me like I'm crazy but I can't help myself. Since my 'Little Katie' lives in me, I want to do things out of the ordinary. And that tells me she was a special little girl. She wants me to let you know she's fine. She loves you and wants you to have a great Christmas because she's having the time of her life."

Mallorie was born on December 2. On her birthday in 2012, Vickie wrote the following tribute to her daughter on her Facebook page. I think this is a fitting way to reflect on the capacity of the heart to love and a testimony to the relationship between a mother and her daughter.

Happy birthday, Mallorie Kate. It is hard to believe that you have been in heaven longer than you were on this earth. How different you are seeing your birthday now in eternity. Here we think of it as another year of getting older, or presents, a big party . . . things that the flesh looks forward to. You already know what your true birthday is. The day you went back into the hands of the One who formed you in my womb. Heaven is your true home. It is your forever birth place, and time is not measured there. You cannot know the days, or the hours you have been missed. There is inexpressible joy in heaven, so you aren't aware that you are missing me. Your joy has been made complete because you have seen Jesus. But there is coming a day when we will meet in that beautiful place. I will see you come running and laughing. You will want to show me everything. I can hear Jesus laughing as well . . . telling me to go on without you, and didn't I remember what a stubborn streak you have; that you were going to show me all the miraculous things you have seen and heard. When this day comes, time won't mean anything to me as well. I will see you, and Mama and Daddy, and many other relatives and friends. We will gather together and rejoice by the river that flows by the throne of God. Until that moment I will miss you and always wonder what your life would have been like here on earth. This is just the way mamas are. The Lord understands this as well. He continues to comfort me and give me peace each day. He gives me joy in my heart in spite of my sorrow. He keeps a song of praise on my lips because of His great love for you and for me. I know you are in His house now. Who better to have raised you during those teenage years than Jesus!! You are truly a daughter of the King! I am thankful and blessed to have been chosen to be your mama. It was for a short while, but the memories are for a lifetime. Our time together again will be forever. I love you hon.

Happy Birthday with love, Mama

CHAPTER 15

RUSH TO REST

There's no other place that I'd rather be
Than kneeling down before my Holy King
In Your presence there is perfect peace
I will rush to rest at Your feet, Lord Jesus.

—"Rush to Rest"

Most of us know the story of Mary and Martha and their brother Lazarus recorded in the Gospels, and how close they were to Jesus. He and His disciples entered Jerusalem and made their way to the small village of Bethany to hang out with the two sisters and their brother and rest after a long day of traveling. We all know it wasn't uncommon for Jesus to walk twenty- to twenty-five miles a day teaching and ministering to anyone who would follow along and listen to Him.

Martha greeted Jesus and his disciples and welcomed them into her home. Once they all took a seat, she went to work, scurrying about to cook dinner for her guests and make sure everything was "just right." She was practical and efficient, and did exactly what most of us would do if a close friend walked into our home—she became consumed by the busyness of preparation and hospitality.

In the meantime, her younger sister Mary sat at Jesus's feet, listening to Him as He talked with Lazarus and the disciples. Mary's apparent laziness bothered Martha tremendously, so she complained to Jesus, who simply told her that Mary was doing what was right. In tender, loving words, Jesus basically told Martha, *I really do appreciate the fact that you are working so diligently because I know you love me. But the thing is, sometimes I'd just like you to sit with Me and listen to Me. Remember, I have the bread of life and it lasts forever. Right now, Mary has chosen to be strengthened by what only I can offer. Why don't you come sit with us? You want to rush around just doing stuff and I just want you to rest. Why don't you rush to rest at My feet?*

I don't know that those were His exact words, but I can imagine He could have that same conversation with all of us. We all have a little of Mary and Martha in us. The practical and diligent side of us keeps us so busy that we neglect spending the time with our Lord, Who we need to sustain us, strengthen us, and help us be more like Him. But then we have the Mary side in us that yearns to be with Him and learn from Him . . . and be loved on by Him. It's a constant inward struggle for us, because it's more difficult to "be still and know" (Psalm 46:10) than it is to be busy and go.

In October 2002, I found myself struggling under some extraordinary circumstances. Time was drawing near for me to write six songs that would be part of LifeWay's "Far Out Far East Rickshaw Rally" VBS. But I had also come back from a concert tour in Italy to find that my father had been placed in hospice care. My flight had barely taxied to the gate when Mama called and said, "You need to come home. Your daddy is really sick."

The songs were due on October 31, but I went to Carrollton to be with my daddy. Part of caring for him involved staying up through the night to massage his legs, which were wracked with pain, and helping him get to the bathroom. So by the time a few days had passed, I had slept very little. On the 29th, two days before the songs were due, I was exhausted. I felt like I needed to let my team at LifeWay know about our circumstances, so I called to fill them in and left a message with one of the team leaders. "I know the songs are due Thursday, but I haven't been able to sit down and work on any of them," I informed him. "My dad's in a really bad place, and I had to come home this week. I know if I could have another week I can get them done. But, today, I don't have anything."

Later that afternoon, that team leader left a message on my phone. "Jeff, I'm sorry for the predicament you are in, but we have to have these songs by Thursday morning."

I called back immediately and got his voicemail. "I don't think you understood my message," I pleaded. "I don't have anything, not even a snippet, and I don't know when I'm going to have a chance to write. But," I paused, "if you're telling me I have to be there Thursday, then I'll be there."

I couldn't simply pack up and leave Mama and Daddy, so I stayed another day, and by the time I left Wednesday night and pointed my car east toward Nashville, I didn't have any idea how I was going to get six songs written in less than twelve hours.

I was ticked. The thought of leaving my parents behind with tears streaming from their eyes collided with how in the world I was going to complete the impossible by 9:00 a.m. the next morning. Normally when I started writing VBS songs, I would first research the culture and music of the region the team had selected. For the "Far Out Far East Rickshaw Rally," it would be helpful to know something about Japanese culture, but I hadn't had the time, so I knew Thursday morning was going to be the start of a very long and painful day.

It takes two hours to get to Memphis from my parents' house, and another three from there to get to Nashville. I drove off into the night mentally kicking and screaming like a little kid. A mile or two down the road I decided I was going to have a "Come to Jesus" meeting with . . . um . . . Jesus. I ranted and raved and fussed with the Lord. I just knew that by the time I got to LifeWay the next morning, it was all gonna be over, because when I walked in there with nothing but a stupid grin on my face, they'd be calling someone else to write those songs.

By the time my wheels hit the Memphis pavement and I merged onto I-40E bound for Nashville, God must have figured I'd had ample time to finish pitching my fit. And in the same gentle voice His Son spoke to Martha, God calmed me down and told me, *If you'll just be quiet and listen to Me, I will write these songs for you.*

I did the only thing I knew to do. I gave up. I took a deep breath, quit all the fussing, and just got quiet. It wasn't long before a pentatonic type melody began to play in my head . . . Da dada DEE da (that's the best way I can mimic the Koto, an Asian instrument, in print). *Hey, that sounds Japanese,* I thought.

And so began the pen of God writing the VBS ballad "Rush to Rest" in my heart. I had wanted to write a song based on Jesus's encounter with Mary and Martha, and here it was. I had that vision of Martha rushing all over the house trying to get everything done, and Mary coming in and running to the feet of Jesus. At that moment, I felt the Lord say, *Rush to me right now. Sit down and listen to Me.* Finally, I resigned myself to His command, and in the car between Memphis and Nashville, I wrote "Rush to Rest" and "Ready for the Race." When I got home, I felt the Lord tell me to go to bed and rest, then get up at 5:00 a.m. So that's what I did.

When I woke up that morning and sat down to write, the Lord gave me the other four songs, "The Rickshaw Rally Theme Song," "Sing a Song of ABC," "Change Me Jesus," and "Run to the One," in just three hours. He had literally whispered them in my ear, and they were written. I was overwhelmed by what He had done.

When I walked into the LifeWay meeting room with the VBS team, I was carrying six completed songs in my folder. Normally, when I played songs for them, they would offer feedback. They might hear something we needed to reword, or change, or completely rework. There always seemed to be at least something they wanted to tweak to make it the best song it could be. But that didn't happen on that Thursday morning.

I played the first song. The team leader looked around the group. "I think that's good. Does anyone have any comments?" No one said anything. "Okay, then, go on."

I played the second song. They looked at each other, their pens still lying on their notebooks. "Anyone want to make any changes to that one? No? We're good on that one."

After the third song, it was the same reaction. I thought, *This is crazy.*

By the time I got to "Rush to Rest," I was wailing inside because I couldn't contain my joy. The Lord did this for me. He did just what He said he would. He gave me all of this, and they weren't making a single change. When I played the last note of "Rush to Rest," everybody smiled. "Jeff, those are great. We love those songs."

The team leader who had left the message forty-eight hours earlier looked at me with a sheepish grin. "I thought you said you didn't have any songs."

"Brother," I said, "I didn't . . . until last night and this morning. The Lord delivered me."

I know now why God gave me "Rush to Rest." While I was working on my *Under God* project, which was released in 2012, and was on my way to the studio, I felt the Lord telling me to honor Daddy by putting that song on the record. Though it had been written some eleven years before that record was put together, it reminded me of that time of chaos and frustration, and how the Lord calmed me down and loved me in a tender way. Each time I hear it, I am reminded of how He provides for me when I simply stop, sit at his feet quietly, and allow Him to do what He already wants to do anyway.

CHAPTER 16

VERO È

THE COUNT OF MONTE CRISTO IS AN ENDURING STORY OF CONFLICT, betrayal, revenge, and romance in which a man, Edmond Dantès, is falsely accused of a crime and subsequently imprisoned for many years. Over time, when at the height of his circumstances he has begun to waver in his faith, an imprisoned priest tries to encourage him, even unto his dying breath. Eventually, Edmund has fallen to one of his lowest points of despair, and cries out to the priest, "I don't believe in God!" In the final moment of his life, the dying priest whispers, "It doesn't matter. He believes in you."

The first time I watched the movie, that particular verbal exchange made an impact on me. Now anytime I see the title, my mind instantly goes back to that powerful scene. Funny how little "moments" in a movie can touch one so deeply that, sometimes, they actually play out in real life as well. For me, I never dreamed of it playing out on a train in the Tuscan hills of Italy.

I had travelled to Italy with my friends from First Baptist Church in Palmetto, Florida, in 1999 to lead worship and perform concerts in open-air piazzas, which resemble park-like squares in the middle of towns, where people gather to decompress after work and enjoy a gelato. A year later, it was in Palmetto, on that pier overlooking the bay, that I wrote "It's All True."

As we performed in different cities along the way, I remember wishing that we had learned our songs in Italian so that people could really grab the message we were trying to convey. I knew that when I got home, I would work hard and be prepared so that the next time I traveled there, I would be able to sing everything in Italian.

There was something about Italy and its people that gripped me. Following that first trip, God gave me this love for them and a burden for the country that so captured my heart I couldn't stop thinking about it. As soon as I stepped out of the airplane and back onto American soil, I couldn't wait to go back.

It just so happened that, timing wise, I wasn't able to return until September 21, 2001—exactly ten days after 9/11—and again in 2002. By that time, having spent a year studying at the Tennessee Foreign Language Institute in Nashville, I had learned my songs in Italian prior to my third trip. Now, I wasn't exactly fluent in Italian, but I was functional enough to be able to sing and communicate the message in a way that could reach all those people milling around the piazzas. I was especially excited to sing the translated version of "It's All True," which, in Italian, is rendered *Vero è*.

By the time we were making our fourth trip, we had a pretty good feel for that part of Italy surrounding the region of Tuscany. In beautiful towns like Florence, Perugia, and Siena, the culture of Italy is rich, and the beauty of the country seems so pure and untouched. From Palazzo Vecchio and Ponte Vecchio, a Medieval stone-arched bridge which overlooks the Arno River, to the dome that sits atop the famous and beautiful

Santa Maria Novella Church, there are breathtaking views of landscape and architecture, as well as magnificent sparkling bodies of water.

So, in 2004 we were there to do a conference and travel all around those places leading worship. We also travelled to the southern region of the country to perform in Naples (Napoli). Naples is the third largest municipality in Italy and well known for many cultural innovations, including being the birthplace of both pizza and the mandolin. Its architecture is steeped in Medieval, Renaissance, and Baroque styles in the many castles, classical ruins, and churches that dot the landscape. With such a backdrop, one can imagine the surprise and amusement we experienced when we noticed that a huge tent had been erected with a stage underneath. But it wasn't the tent or the stage that amused us; it was the fact that these people had set up 2,000 seats for the anticipated crowd. *Seriously?* I thought, *There isn't a soul around here who's ever heard of the four of us, and you're out of your mind if you think twenty people—much less 2,000—are coming to hear some brother from Nashville, Tennessee, butcher his choruses because he's trying to sing them in Italian.* And it was a two-night event. However, unbeknownst to us, a CD the four of us had recorded in Italian two years prior had trickled its way throughout the Italian "boot."

Apparently, Christian radio stations all over Italy had been playing our CD, especially "Vero è" and "Se Mi Affido" ("As I Wait") and it became clear to me, as 2,000 people stood up to sing "Vero è" with me, that the Lord had been working behind the scenes . . . as He does so constantly in all of our lives. These people we had fallen in love with had been listening to our songs on the radio. Not just mine, but songs from Leann Albrecht, Patti Franklin, and David McKay. Hearing our songs sung with such conviction in another language was one of my life's sweetest surprises. Within those worshipful moments, I pictured the Lord bending down and kissing me on the forehead, just like a loving father does his little boy. Both nights we played to standing-room-only crowds, before traveling back north to Florence.

On the afternoon between those concerts, we visited an elementary school in Caserta, Italy, where the teacher had her fourth-grade class sing to me. I can't even begin to describe the sound coming from that room as they sang "Vero è." It was as touching a moment as I have ever experienced. I stood there and wept, because I was thinking about the long and arduous journey of this song.

From the time the Lord had planted the seed for that song in my heart on the day my dad first got his diagnosis, to the day I wrote the song on the pier in Palmetto Bay, "It's All True" had crossed so many boundaries. It was one of those Ebenezer moments, because that song is as personal a one as I have ever written, or will ever write—it is a song born out of pain, yet filled with hope and great joy—much like the pruning God does in our lives. It's painful, yes, but it brings much fruit.

The next day, we traveled back to the Tuscan hills to spend a few days with our good friend, Giorgio Ammirabile, and his dear parents, Giovanni and Grazia. While there, we were preparing for the Christian Artists Festival. We had a couple of days off while artists began to arrive and final preparations were made for the conference. So, six of us—Leann Albrecht, Linda Forrest, David and Betty McKay, Dawn Werner, and myself—decided to go to Siena. Siena means "red" in Italian, most likely because of the reddish clay that surrounds the town. Little did I know how profound that color would become.

Giorgio thought it would be best for us to take a bus to Poggibonsi, which would connect us with the bus that would take us on to Siena.

But, Poggibonsi—as far from metropolitan as one could get and where chickens clucked all around—seemed to be the "point of no return" for us, at least for that day, for when we got off the bus, we discovered that no other buses would be leaving until the next day at three o'clock in the afternoon.

Trying to absorb what was happening, while also attempting to formulate a plan to get back to Giorgio and his family, we walked over to a nearby store to buy some water. Propped against the doorway leading inside the store was this beautiful, dark-haired woman, wearing a dress that seemed like it was made from 100 scarves flowing gently in the wind. Her dress seemed to match her personality as a free spirit. She smiled easily and told us the store was closed for a bit. "The workers are on siesta, and they will reopen in a couple of hours."

By speaking English, she quickly became our newest BFF. She explained in great detail how we could purchase tickets at a nearby travel agency. She pointed us in the right direction, but that wasn't enough. "You'll go down this street two blocks. Turn left. On that street, in the second building on the left, you'll find a travel agency, which sells tickets for the train. The train station offices are closed, so you have to buy your tickets there. When you leave, you'll go down a hill on the same street and run into the train station. The train for Siena leaves at four o'clock."

"You seem to know so much about this city," I said, completely overwhelmed by the wealth of knowledge she possessed of a transit system in a city she was merely "visiting." In her unassuming way, she diverted my comment by explaining she was visiting a friend and was waiting to be picked up, and that she was on her way out of town to go back home to Los Angeles. Her name was Jordan.

Incredulously, I couldn't help myself. "How long have you been here?"

She was nonchalant. "Oh, a couple of days."

Feeling a supernatural element in the air, I happened to glance past Jordan and looked into Betty's eyes, as big as saucers, and realized she was silently mouthing, *Jor-dan Ri-ver! Ci-ty of Ang-els!* She was beginning to understand, as we all were, the Biblical connection between her name, her American hometown, and the guardian angel–like characteristics she emanated. It was all way more than simple coincidence, far beyond the realm of happenstance.

I noticed that she had no purse. She had no luggage. She carried nothing; she didn't even have pockets. "Where is all your stuff?" I asked her. She smiled knowingly, almost winking, and said, "I travel light." It was as if she relished the fact that we were catching on to this divine exchange between us.

We stood speechless as she turned and walked away.

AFTER A SHORT TRAIN RIDE, WE FINALLY MADE IT TO SIENA. COMING OUT of the station we approached what my southern roots would describe as a boulevard. This boulevard followed the ancient stone wall that surrounded the city. The walk was downhill, and there were places in the wall that provided gaps where tourists could take in the breathtaking vistas of the surrounding mountains, ancient relics, and the oncoming sunset.

My friend Leann loves to take pictures, especially at sunset, and because we were arriving at that time of day, she was beside herself. She is always talking about perspective, and every few steps seemed to provide her with enough "perspective" to stop and snap another photograph, or seven. So as we came into Siena, she got us all posed for a group picture before she'd let us move on and do the sightseeing we came to do. We were also looking for a good restaurant. It had been a long time since lunch.

Rush hour in Siena, Italy, is a lot like rush hour anywhere else in the world, and by the time five o'clock rolled around and our "photo shoot" at the boulevard ended, we found ourselves in a horde of traffic and humanity.

It had been about fifteen minutes since we left the boulevard and strolled through the ancient entrance to the city, which is adjacent to a large roundabout where traffic flows like water through a fire hose. We were laughing and enjoying the moment when, all of a sudden, a look of horror came on Leann's face and she stopped dead in her tracks. She touched her shoulder and screamed, "My purse!" In an instant, all of our hearts sank at once—partly because of the look on her face and partly because all six of us left without realizing the purse had been forgotten at one of the many stops along the boulevard. As if shot out of a cannon, Leann was off, backtracking to possible places she may have left the purse. As she moved frantically, she fired off a list of items that were in her purse: "Both our passports . . . both our wallets . . . (pant pant) . . . all our cash . . . all our euros . . . (pant pant) . . . Carl's gonna kill me!" Thank God, at that very moment, her husband Carl was spending a leisurely afternoon with other musicians Gary Lunn and Mike and Nancy Demus back at Poggio Ubertini, unaware of the chaos that had just ensued. To put it mildly, his German DNA would have made it difficult for him to embrace this situation well.

Running right behind Leann, I was thinking of solutions if we didn't find this red purse. I figured we would end up at the American Embassy to sort it all out, because without that purse and all its contents, there was no way she and Carl were getting home.

At that point, we were at the roundabout, waiting for the first gap in traffic to dart through to the other side. Finally, one car graciously slowed enough to allow us to cross in front of it. But, immediately, the driver began honking at us. I thought, *He let us cross in front of him, so why's he so angry and honking his horn?* Several times he honked his horn and was waving his hands at us. We turned and continued running, until we heard him yell, "Borsa! Borsa!" We froze when we heard that word because we instantly knew he had just said, "Purse!"

That one word seemed to stop the entire world. Leann and I both turned and saw the man's wife, in the backseat next to her baby, holding up Leann's red purse. It had been a full twenty minutes, and traffic was flowing so fast that my mind could not comprehend how this couple could have possibly stopped to find the red purse, pick it up, know whose it was, and begin to enter the city when they encountered us at that roundabout. I felt like we were in a dream sequence, where everything was in slow motion as we approached the car. We were in the middle of the street, and cars were whizzing by on one side and honking at a dead still behind this car. The driver stepped out of the car and handed Leann her purse. He didn't say a single word, and his wife was waving, bowing, and blowing kisses at us.

Leann and I hugged the man, smiled and waved at the baby, and thanked them profusely. I offered him 20 euros, but he refused and returned to his car to drive away. Quickly, the natural flow of traffic resumed. In just a few moments we went from the pit of despair to the peak of elation.

Leann and I crossed the street to meet up with the others. The expression on her face relayed the depth of this indescribable series of events that had played out before us. "Can anyone explain what just happened here?" Leann asked breathlessly. Because no one could, we decided to do the only thing we knew. We held hands and had a prayer of thanksgiving and worshipped the Lord for reminding us of His protection and faithfulness.

We finally made our way into the city. The odd thing was, we had spent the entire day wearing ourselves out to get to Siena, and we were still reeling from laughter from the whole "Borsa" experience when someone asked a simple, yet profound, question: "So, why did we want to come here?" The question hit us all like a cup of cold water in the face. There was such a driving force pushing us to this place. We had been so excited about getting there, and in an instant we realized none of us had a clue why we were there. We didn't know the first thing about Siena; no one in our group could name the first landmark, ancient church, museum, or famous statue.

We began to walk through a park when I noticed a lady holding a red purse similar to Leann's. I felt the Lord say, "Go and talk to her. She knows what you're supposed to do next." To prevent her from being startled, I asked Leann to walk over with me. We approached, and I asked, "Parli Inglese?"

"Yes."

"We are from the United States," I said. "We came here to Siena but really don't know what to do. Could you recommend some places for us to go?" She smiled and seemed to relish the opportunity to map out everything for us to do the rest of that day. She gave us precise directions where to go to see particular buildings, parks, and museums of interest and even to a restaurant in the Piazza de Campo called Il Mangia. "You'll love it," she assured us.

Even with her directions, we got turned around at one point. A photographer from Washington State, on sabbatical there for a year, approached us and asked if we were lost and needed help. We told him we were looking for the Il Mangia restaurant, and he pointed us in the right direction. He told us we were close and that we would absolutely love it.

Oh, and did I mention that he was wearing a red shirt?

Il Mangia was everything our "angel in disguise" had promised. Our meal and the service we received exceeded all our expectations, and we fully savored every moment around that table. By the time we noticed the clock was creeping toward 9:00 p.m., we were beginning to wonder how we were going to get back to Giorgio's place. A train was leaving in an hour, but we had no clue what connections we were going to have to take or even how to get to his house once we got back to Tuscany. I called his home, and his mother Grazia answered the phone. However, between the static, her high-speed Italian, and my not-so-perfect interpretational skills, I was unable to help her understand our predicament. Florence was about an hour from Giorgio's house, and we could get that far; but from there we had no idea how we were going to negotiate the rest of the trip.

But we boarded a train, nonetheless. Based on our crazy day, the Lord obviously had more adventures in store.

David sat down next to a handsome, young Italian man. However, everything about him screamed "Leave me alone!" His eyes were dark and cold and fixed. His chiseled face reflected a deep scowl. So, naturally, the deep Delta roots in me kicked in, and with a smile as wide as the Mississippi River, I engaged him in conversation. "*Buono seraaaaa!*" And, just as I had asked the lady with the red purse earlier, "Parli Inglese?"

He glared at me for the first time. "*No!* Italiano!" Every bit of his body language was begging me to leave him alone. Undaunted by his terse response, my determination was fueled by the idea that we were going to be BFFs before I got off that train.

"*Como ti chiamo?*"

"Rudolfo." He barely glanced at me.

"*Che cosa lavora fa?*" I asked, thinking I was inquiring about his occupation. However, what I think I actually asked him was, "What does work?" He just rolled his eyes.

I continued to grill him with questions in Italian, and in the long process I finally discovered he was a policeman. Eventually, I decided to give him a brief respite before continuing to build our obviously budding relationship.

I turned my attention back to my friends and began regaling them with a story about Ron Shuff's dance band in Nashville with which I had worked a great deal back in the 1990s. Appearance-wise, we would have been mistaken for the Lawrence Welk band. Raise your hand if your mother, like mine, forced you to watch the *Lawrence Welk Show* on Saturday nights. With Dippity-Do dripping from their hair, my sisters would squeal in pain as my mother would pop them in the head with the hair brush. "Be still! I'm trying to listen," she would order as Lawrence conducted his big band while my mom worked their Sunday-go-to-meeting hair and made sure I had enough Kiwi polish to spit-shine my shoes.

But I digress.

The dance band covered everything from Big Band to Motown and all the most popular party songs. One night, while playing a country club reception, Ron called up "The Macarena." As the band pulled up the charts, I noticed there was no lyric sheet. As Ron began to kick off the number, I frantically whispered, "I can't find the lyric sheet!" He glanced over his shoulder just before the down beat and flippantly said, "Make 'em up."

I shudder to think how offended any Hispanic person in attendance might have felt as I called up every simple Spanish word I learned watching *Sesame Street* as a kid and repeated them over and over throughout the song. They must have wondered why I kept saying, "water," "good day," "how are you?" and why I kept counting to twenty.

Meanwhile, back on the train . . . as my friends were laughing throughout the conversation, my new Italian "amico" started to laugh as well. I looked at him and said, "*Sono pazzo!*" ("I'm crazy!"). Then, in perfect English, he responded, "You're a singer?"

"Yes, I am."

"What do you sing?"

"Christian, evangelical music."

"Oh. Well, you don't want to talk to me." He raised his hand to slightly cover his face.

"Why would you say that?"

"Because I'm a bad person."

"What makes you think you're a bad person?"

"Because I believe in God, but I don't believe in church."

Instantly, I was thrust inside the prison cell of the Count of Monte Cristo as the priest to Rudolfo's Edmond Dantès. And I heard myself say, "I'm glad you believe in God. He believes in you."

Instantly those hard eyes softened.

"A lot of people don't believe in church, because they've been hurt by the church," I continued, feeling that familiar nudge from the Lord, sensing Him directing my words. "I was hurt in church too, Rudolfo. I went through a time when I felt the same as you. But, listen. I'm not going to quote a lot of scriptures to you or tell you why you should trust God or love Him. I'm just going to tell you why I do." I began to talk about how faithful the Lord had been to me in my life.

Eventually, I shared with him all that the Lord had done just that day to prove how much He cared about us: the bus ride, Jordan from Los Angeles, Leann's red purse, the woman with the red purse in the park, the photographer with the red shirt from Washington . . . all the connections throughout the day that got us where we were at that moment.

There was no doubt Who was orchestrating the whole thing, probably just for the sole purpose of us meeting Rudolfo. How else can you explain God using the color red in some form all along the way in a town whose name literally means "Red"?

"Throughout the entire day, God was working things out for us," I told him.

Rudolfo listened intently, but refused to believe the story about the red purse. "You lie," he barked. "This could not happen. You're making this up!"

At the precise moment that I affirmed to him I was telling the truth, the conductor of the train came walking through our car with a cell phone in his hand. And he was calling my name. "Jeff Slaughter? Jeff Slaughter?" Shocked, I raised my hand, and he handed me his cell phone.

The voice on the other end said, "Jeff, it's Giovanni. Where are you?"

"On a train headed to Florence." My head was swimming at all that had happened. I couldn't possibly fathom an answer, and I didn't even know how, in that moment, I was cognizant enough to carry on a conversation. How did Giovanni possibly find this particular cell number, on this particular route, and how did the conductor find me in this particular compartment of a fifty-car train?

"Do you stop in Empoli?" Giovanni asked.

I asked the conductor and he said, "Five minutes."

Giovanni said he was already in Empoli. "I will meet you there."

Handing the conductor his phone with my heart about to explode, I looked right at Rudolfo. "See, that is what I'm talking about."

Rudolfo's tone, although broken, was now gentle. "I have never seen this happen on a train."

"That's how He takes care of us. He wants to take care of you, too," I said. "My friends and I didn't know why we went to Siena today. But now I know. God set up this whole day for me to meet you and to tell you how much He loves you. I want to pray for you, that you would understand more about the love of the Lord. Would it embarrass you if I prayed for you right now?"

"No . . . I like."

So, I prayed for my new friend. As soon as I said, "Amen," the train stopped. And our day's mission was accomplished, even if we didn't recognize it until that moment. I hugged Rudolfo and walked off the train, where Giovanni and Giorgio were waiting for us.

But the Lord still had one more surprise.

Giovanni and Grazia did not have a car, and even when the phone call came, I wondered how they'd gotten to Empoli. I just assumed they'd taken a bus. As we walked through the train station, Giovanni was gushing. With his heavy, almost indiscernible accent, he said, "You never believe what happen today. This man stop at my house and give me this car." He pointed over to a black sedan.

The funny thing is, I had no trouble believing him at all. Years later, my friend Linda found a picture she had taken of me sharing that prayer with Rudolfo. Imagine how I felt when I noticed the shirt I was wearing was . . . red.

CHAPTER 17

REDEEM THE DAY

I AM NO GEOGRAPHY EXPERT, BUT I DO KNOW THAT THERE IS A LOT OF land and even more water between Naples, Italy, and Pueblo, Colorado. In fact, there are 2,268 land miles and 3,490 miles across the Atlantic Ocean, give or take, between the two.

But in just a few months' time in 2004, my "chance" meeting on that Italian train and a phone call in the semi-arid desert land of Pueblo caused the span between the two to close significantly. And that's when I came to understand how the scope of distance shrinks when I consider it from God's perspective.

Within two weeks of returning from Italy, our bass player Gary received devastating news: His precious wife June was battling Stage 4 breast cancer, a vicious type that had metastasized and had begun eating away the bone in her spine. Because of the severity of her case, the oncologist didn't offer any sort of chemotherapy or radiation protocol. Yet, with unwavering faith, they left his office realizing the Lord had a different plan. He began to reveal to them that this battle would be fought and won through the prayers and fasting of family and close friends.

There is a deep, spiritual place one must draw from in order to pray those kinds of prayers and fast for others. It is an intimate place. It is a vulnerable place. It is a place only known by those who have spent considerable time with the Lord and have balanced heartache and faith in a way that can be explained only by that deep and personal relationship with Him.

Knowing that, I confess that it was hard for me to return to that place with the Lord so shortly after my father had lost his battle with cancer. It was difficult for me to go there again because my faith to believe in a miraculous healing of cancer was below "zero." But after I spent time reflecting on what God had shown me just a few weeks before in Italy, I finally got to a point where I could try again.

There was one particular realization that helped the most: Gary and his wife were willing to go there despite the dire prognosis, and they wanted—needed—their friends to stand with them and walk beside them, praying and fasting. "Lord," I said, "I love Gary and June and they've asked me to do this, so I will. And I love You and I sense that You're asking me to do this, so I will. Just give me the strength to believe and trust You with the results."

It was a moment similar to the scripture in Mark 9 where Jesus told a man that all things were possible with faith. The man's son was overcome with an evil spirit, and that father, out of fear, frustration, and desperation, cried out to Jesus, "I do believe; help me overcome my unbelief."

As I prayed, I got the idea to start a "list of miracles" in a journal-type book. In that book, I was going to record miracles I felt I should pray for and believe in, and document when those miracles came to fruition. My miracle request for June was the first—and at that point, only—listing in the book. Her name on that list reminded me every day to pray for her healing, while our group of friends rotated taking days to fast.

By 2005, I was travelling with Kim Hill playing keyboard and singing backup for her as she led worship. We were at a conference in Laguna
Beach, California, in February, where Rick Warren was speaking at the
annual meeting of the "Young Professionals Organization." On the last
day of the conference, Kim and I decided to take a mid-morning walk
on the beach. The breeze coming off the water was crisp and refreshing.
It was the kind of walk where, even though you are with someone, it is
mostly quiet as you find yourself lost in your own thoughts.

As we finished our walk and approached the entrance to the hotel, we
stopped to wash the sand from our feet when we noticed a young couple
sitting on a nearby bench enjoying the quietness of the morning. By the
way they were interacting with each other, it was obvious they were soaking in every moment.

"Hey, how are ya'll this morning?" I asked.

"We're blessed," they smiled.

"Well, we are, too . . . and you're Christians, aren't you?"

"Yes, we are." Their demeanor and sweet love for each other was contagious. "How could you tell?"

"Because you said you were blessed, and most people don't use that
phrase to describe how they are. And, I can just tell by your counte-
nance."

Kim and I parted ways to go back to our rooms and pack before
checking out. A little later, I walked back toward the lobby and looked
out over the adjacent patio area. The whole back wall of the hotel consisted of windows so that guests could bask in the spectacular view of the
Pacific Ocean. The patio just outside provided a perfect refuge to sit in
silence and take in the surroundings.

"Hey, again," I said when I saw the same couple on the patio. They must have been amused by this Mississippi boy always popping up wherever they were sitting.

They smiled back, which obviously meant they were extending an invitation for me to come and chat for a while. So, as I went to sit down, I heard Nichole tell her husband, Tim, "I feel like we should tell him about your situation." They began to explain to me that Tim had liver cancer. It had progressed to the point of measuring life by "good days" and "bad days." On the good days, "we love to come here and allow the beauty of this place to encourage us to keep holding on," Nichole explained. They didn't mention the bad days.

"Tim," I said, "a couple of years ago, I walked through a cancer situation with my dad, so I understand what it means to savor the good days. I can relate to the road you're walking."

I also told them about June and that I had a list of miracles that I kept with me. This list contained the names of people going through things like this. "So far," I smiled at him, "there is exactly one person on my list, and I just found my second." I looked him directly in the eye and said, "Tim, I'm going to commit to pray for you every single day until we see your healing come to pass. I'd like to keep up with you on a weekly basis to see how your treatments are going and continue to know how I can specifically pray for you. I'm believing for a miracle in your life."

For a couple of years, March 18 had been a dark day for me. Whenever I thought of that day, I would be reminded of the evening hours when an internal shaking of the foundation of my faith began. It was the night I realized that my daddy's death was inevitable, and I had been praying and begging for a miracle that was not going to come. I was numb and helpless. I didn't understand what I felt, except that it seemed as if God was letting me down. I could literally feel my heart hardening toward Him. The very number of the day itself is seemingly full of contradiction. On the one hand, the Biblical meaning behind the number eighteen means "bondage," while on the other, it means "life." At this moment, life—on earth or in Heaven—meant very little to me, mostly because I was in the grip of sorrow.

On that night, I remember a storm raging outside. Thunder roared, lightning streaked across the sky, and winds howled. The tempest outside perfectly mirrored the storm seething within me. That foundation of faith was coming apart at the seams because I had read the hospice manuals, and I knew the facts. I knew how to recognize all those "signs of imminent death" when they began to transpire. I felt like I was suffocating. My whole life with my daddy was flashing before my eyes, and now this chapter of life was about to end; no more Christmases, or birthdays, or Sunday afternoon lunches around the family table. . . .

There were so many layers to uncover, and it just kept getting sadder and sadder. I was responding to God like a child who kicks and screams when he doesn't get his way. I was mad because He wasn't answering my prayers the way I wanted Him to, yet sad because of the way I felt toward Him. It was a Jacob-like wrestling match I was having with God. The next morning in the shower I even said to Him, "Here's the deal," as if I had some kind of control. Every time March 18 came around, I was bitterly reminded that when I had needed Him to do it the most, when I had prayed the hardest, God had chosen not to "move that mountain" for me.

A MONTH AFTER I MET TIM AND NICHOLE IN CALIFORNIA, I WAS DOING a LifeWay event with David Platt in Glorietta, New Mexico, after which we were both headed to Pueblo, Colorado, for two separate events. I don't need to tell you, but David Platt can *preach*, and by 2007, he became the teaching pastor at the Church of Brook Hills in Birmingham, Alabama, the youngest mega-church pastor in America.

Glorietta to Pueblo is about a four-hour drive. At some point during the trip, my phone rang, and my friend Linda Forrest from Nashville was on the other end.

"Hello?" I answered. Luckily, David was driving.

"Jeff?" I could barely hear her, because there was so much noise. There was clearly some kind of great party going on on the other end.

"What? I can't hear you! What's going on?!" I shouted as David glanced over with an expression that read, *Is everything okay?*

Finally, Linda must have walked into another room so that I could hear her more clearly. As we crossed over from New Mexico into Colorado, with the bright blue sky and terra cotta backdrop of land trumpeting the beautiful mid-morning sunshine, Linda could hardly contain herself. Obviously, this was *some* kind of party going on back in Nashville.

"You won't believe what happened!" she said breathlessly. "June had scans done this week. They got the results back, and the doctor told her she is cancer free!"

All at the same time, I was gasping, laughing, rocking, crying, bouncing . . . and David was simultaneously shooting concerned glances at me and trying to keep his eyes on the road. "Are you kidding? Thank you, Lord!" I was as breathless as Linda now.

"And Jeff, that's not all," she said, the celebration behind her as strong as ever. "Where the bone in her spine had been eaten away, there is new bone in its place. The doctor has declared June's case a 'complete miracle.'"

As long as I live, the laughter and sounds of celebration on the other end of that phone will be some of the sweetest I have ever heard.

After Linda hung up, I was finally able to tell David what had happened—how June was offered no sort of treatment, and how God had miraculously worked through the prayers and fasting of His people.

After about ten minutes, my phone rang again.

"Jeff . . . hey, this is Tim." This was the man I had met in California. There was a sweet excitement in his voice. "Jeff, you won't believe what happened today," Tim said. Although there wasn't as much noise in the background, he was every bit as giddy as Linda had been.

"What happened?" I asked, truly hoping what I wanted to hear was indeed what I was about to hear.

"I had scans done earlier this week and just got the results back," Tim said. "They were clear, and the doctor said I am cancer-free! Jeff, the doctor looked at me and said, 'It's a miracle.' It's a miracle, Jeff. A miracle!"

I told him about June, and he chuckled, "Well, I guess now we'll have to find some new names for your list."

As I looked out the window, listening to the hum of the engine and the *thumpthumpthump* of the tires rolling over the highway, I realized what date it was: March 18. For a few years, it had been a date that was so dark and painful for me. A date that took me back to that bitter night when I wrestled with God and challenged Him to move a mountain for me. And when He didn't, it angered me. It hurt me.

But, in that moment, I sensed the Lord whispering to me, *It's March 18, Jeff. I have redeemed this day for you now. You won't think about this day the same way ever again.*

And, just because He can, the Lord put an exclamation mark on that redemption when we arrived in Pueblo. David dropped me off at the home of my friends Carl and Melinda Lucero to stay for a couple of days before he and I would fly home. Ten years earlier, Carl and I were running around South Korea worried we'd become street people, which we spent the first hour or so reminiscing and laughing about.

They had planned a cookout with some of friends from their church, so they showed me to an upstairs room where I could freshen up before the get-together. I didn't readily notice the treadmill tucked away in the corner, or the handmade comforter, or the antique furniture that had been passed down through the generations. What I noticed instead would likely have been the most insignificant item to most anybody else: it was the pillow on the bed.

Really, it was banal compared to the rest of the room. It was made for comfort rather than decoration, and it was the exact same type of pillow I had bought my daddy for Christmas before he died. I had racked my brain trying to figure out what to get him for what I realized would be his last Christmas. Since he had been bedridden for the better part of three months, I figured a good Tempur-Pedic pillow would be the best option and would mean the most to him.

It turned out to be the perfect gift, because he loved sleeping on that pillow. It helped him be more comfortable and eased the pain in those last few months of his battle with cancer. He slept on it every night. After he died, and the coroner had taken his body away from the house, I picked that pillow up and held it close, and I remember how it smelled like my daddy. At that moment, it became one of my most cherished possessions, and I immediately took it and sealed it in a bag, hoping that his smell would stay on that pillow forever.

"We thought you'd like to sleep on that pillow. It is so comfortable," Melinda said.

I thought, *You have no idea.* And I was trying not to have a complete meltdown right there in front of them, but I could feel a flood of tears welling up inside me.

Later that evening, as I lay down on the pillow, I felt the memories of a stormy, heart-wrenching night two years before. God was giving me this pillow to sleep on because the next morning would bring with it redemption. I realized God had set up that whole day to bless me and to comfort me.

So now, some ten years later, March 18 holds an entirely different feeling for me. No longer is it as dark and painful. It certainly no longer harbors bitterness or anger or questions about moving mountains. Today, the number eighteen is indeed about life and salvation. Because that day has been redeemed for me. Now, and for the rest of my life, it will be a day of miracles.

CHAPTER 18

WHEN THE DEAD SEA SCROLLS BREATHED LIFE INTO ME

WHILE IT MIGHT BE HARD TO BELIEVE, AS A KID THERE WERE FEW things I dreaded more than Vacation Bible School and summer camp. How about that for irony? But it's true because, for me, VBS and camp were places where I felt least valuable, the least safe, and . . . the most miserable.

Both places provided ample opportunity for other kids to take every advantage of making fun of me. I was overweight, and my mama always cut my hair to save money. She would sit me in a chair in the kitchen and take a comb and a razor blade and start chopping away at my hair, yanking as much out of my scalp as she was actually cutting. If you've never had your hair cut with a razor blade and comb, rest assured it's a painful process. Your hair gets pulled and jerked and chopped, and to make it worse, as Mama took a pair of scissors to even things out around the edges, she always seemed to nick my ear. So many times afterward I sat there with a sore head and a bloody ear. Needless to say, I dreaded haircut day about as much as my sisters looked forward to their Saturday night Dippity Do fiasco.

So, I spent most of my childhood with extra weight and bad haircuts. To top it off, I was as unathletic as one can be and didn't know the first thing about sports, so at VBS recreation time I was called a sissy, and at camp I was never chosen to participate in sporting events. At both, I always felt like an outcast. So, basically, I grew up seeing myself as the loser with the lisp, the bad "mama 'do," and the tuba.

There aren't three bigger strikes against a kid than those.

The only reprieve I had at the time was my piano, my singing, and my Bible. The Bible was a King James Version with a red-leather binding and had my name, "Jeffrey Carl Slaughter," stamped in gold lettering across the bottom of the front cover. My parents gave it to me for Christmas in 1972. While some kids may have been angry with God, I guess I was just confused and wondered what was wrong with me. I had this long shadow of guilt from the embarrassing abuse I had experienced and the even longer darkness that shrouded me because of what my peers thought of me.

Every night before I went to bed, I developed a habit of reading my Bible. It provided the diversion I needed to make it through the next day. I loved delving into the familiar Scriptures and reading about "the least of these" through whom God always seemed to do great things.

One night I came across the book of Habakkuk and thought, *What a weird name.* The name alone drew my attention, and I began to read about this minor prophet. I didn't know it then as a child so much, but I began to realize this beautifully written book in the Old Testament uses two of its three chapters to share Habakkuk's ongoing and powerful dialogue with Yahweh. Habakkuk offered me a beginning point for healing. The first few verses of Habakkuk's first chapter reeled me in because, in a way, Habakkuk's questions of God were the same ones I was asking: "How long, O Lord, must I call for help, but you do not listen? Or cry out to you, 'Violence!' But you do not save? Why do you make me look at injustice? Why do you tolerate wrongdoing? Destruction and violence are before me; there is strife and conflict abounds. Therefore the law is paralyzed, and justice never prevails. The wicked hem in the righteous, so that justice is perverted" (vv. 2–4).

But, then, I was particularly drawn to the second chapter. Habakkuk has asked God some heart-wrenching questions as he aches for his people and anticipates their sin being punished by the oncoming destruction at the hands of the Chaldeans. In the midst of this, the second chapter is the place where Habakkuk braces himself to hear from God, as he stands watch, "stationed on the ramparts" (v. 1). And in a book that starts out with a heart-cry as the precursor to destruction, Habakkuk's writings progress from a shaky faith brimming with perplexity and doubt to the height of absolute trust in God.

Then, I read what almost at once I knew would be the words that would change my life. In verse 2 of that second chapter, God told his prophet to record a vision on his heart and "hold it there, for though it may tarry, it will surely come." Even at such a young age, I felt the Lord was saying to me, *Don't worry about what people say about you. Focus on what I say about you. I have made you to do special things for me. It may take a while for you to see it, but your vision is coming.*

Many years later, in 2008, I got an opportunity to go to the Garden Tomb in Israel to film the VBS music video for "Because," which was going to be the ABC song for Boomerang Express that next summer. The ABC song has always served as the week's main evangelistic message. The letters "ABC" stand for "admit," "believe," and "confess," and these songs talk about what it means to become a believer in Christ through those three steps. Up until that year, I had always written this song in an upbeat, fun, and quirky manner that I thought would attract kids to it even more. At the first meeting we had for Boomerang Express, however, Lynne Norris suggested that I approach it differently that year.

"I'd like for you to try and write it as a ballad," she said, "because, if you're up for it, we'll fly to Israel and film the video in front of the Garden Tomb."

I was blown away. There aren't many people in the world who get to film a video for a song they've written about salvation in the very place where the price for that salvation was paid.

During the filming of the video, we shot footage while in a boat on the Sea of Galilee, where Jesus walked out on the water to meet His disciples during a storm; atop the peaks of the Judean Desert, where Jesus spent forty days fasting and praying before beginning His three-year ministry on earth; on the Mount of Olives overlooking the city of Jerusalem, where Jesus spent the last week of His life with His disciples, the eleven men whose testimonies of their time with Jesus would forever change the course of humankind; and the Garden Tomb, close to Golgotha, where Jesus was crucified, buried, and resurrected.

The stark contrast of terrain that was both beautiful and rugged was a life-changing experience for me. While visiting the places where Jesus had walked, I came to realize how far-reaching His ministry truly was. We spent a lot of time filming at several locations, and I was able to spend some time alone at each one. I got to compare what I had read about Jesus and what I knew about Him from my own experiences. I tried to put myself in those places and imagine what it must have been like to be an onlooker watching Him perform miracles and seeing how

He reached out to touch so many sick and hurting people. He loved them all in such a profound and powerful way.

While we were filming the instructional part of the video where I teach the movements and share the personal stories of those songs, I said on camera, "Other than the day I accepted the Lord, this is the greatest moment of my life, to stand in front of this tomb to teach and sing to you about what the Lord did right here. The emptiness of this tomb is the reason we can have a relationship with Him and receive eternal life."

Along the way, we visited Capernaum, the beautiful town where Jesus lived at the northern side of the Sea of Galilee and the Kidron Valley. Jesus crossed the Kidron Valley, which runs along the eastern wall of Jerusalem, many times during his travels from Jerusalem to Bethany to visit Mary, Martha, and their brother Lazarus.

On the last day of our trip, we went to the Shrine of the Book, which is a wing of the Israel Museum that houses the Dead Sea Scrolls, the oldest writings of the Bible. The Scrolls were first discovered in a cave by a teenaged shepherd in the mid-1940s. Over the next eight years or so, as many as eleven caves produced bits and pieces of the Scrolls in what is now known as the West Bank in Palestine. Altogether, they contain a collection of 972 texts from the Old Testament.

The museum itself is topped by a beautifully constructed white dome that covers a structure that is two-thirds below ground and is reflected in a pool of water that surrounds it. A black basalt wall just outside provides a separation of the museum from a scaled-down model version of Jerusalem and Solomon's Temple, which is surrounded by a four-foot wall.

Seeing Solomon's Temple took me back to my Sunday School days at North Greenwood Baptist Church with Mrs. Gloria Hemmer. Mrs. Hemmer laughed easily but had this authoritative air about her. She was very regal, with large, white, cat-eye glasses and perfectly coiffed jet black hair, and when she stood erect at the podium to teach us, she folded her right hand over her left. She wasn't just any ordinary Sunday School teacher, mind you, because she loved teaching elementary school kids the Bible. And that is also one of the reasons she made such a terrific Vacation Bible School director.

She had divided the Bible into different categories, and expected us to memorize the order of the sixty-six books within. In the Old Testament we would first memorize the Pentateuch (first five books), then the books of history (Joshua to Esther), followed by the books of poetry and wisdom (Job and Song of Solomon), and then all the minor and major prophets (Isaiah to Malachi). In the New Testament, we would start with history (Matthew to Acts), go through the letters (Romans to Jude), and finally end with the apocalypse (Revelation). So serious was Mrs. Hemmer, in fact, that we all had a holy fear we would not be promoted to the next Sunday School grade unless we were able to memorize the order of those sixty-six books by the end of the year.

When you entered Mrs. Hemmer's class as a fourth grader, you were instantly mesmerized by her room. She adored kids, and everyone who ever sat under her instruction knew he or she was loved and valued. She believed every kid could know God in a deep and very personal way.

The reason I was reminded of Mrs. Hemmer at that moment outside the museum of the Shrine of the Book in Israel was that she, too, had this miniature replica of Solomon's Temple. And I can vividly remember all those years later how fascinated I was looking at that temple while she described the Glory Cloud of God that filled that place. My love and appreciation for the Bible is due in large part to her passion for teaching it to us.

Inside the Shrine of the Book in the Israel Museum, in the innermost sanctum, was a round room. Before you got there, though, you could spend lots of time checking out what life was like during Jesus's day. There were numerous artifacts on exhibit, such as clay water pitchers, tools, and even the tubes that had once contained the Dead Sea Scrolls. All were encased behind thick glass. No one was allowed to take pictures of anything in the museum. The lights were dim, which helped to set a solemn, reverent, holy mood. People within the museum were quiet, very much in awe of what they were experiencing.

Once I made my way to the other side of the museum, where that round room awaited, I walked in through a wide threshold where, along the walls, were tall, vertical glass cases about three feet wide and six to eight feet tall that housed other writings and artifacts. In the middle of the round room was where the most ancient artifacts were exhibited. I approached the exhibit by climbing six steps to a round case that looked like a giant, hand-carved, cherry-wood gavel with its handle pointing skyward. The glass case surrounding the gavel was lit, and this is where the oldest of the Dead Sea Scrolls were housed.

Most of the scrolls were made of parchment, while the rest were papyrus and so aged that they had rotted and their edges were dark and jagged. This reminded me of my mom's decoupage projects during the 1970s, where she would take a copy of the Ten Commandments (and anything else she deemed worthy of framing), burn the edges to make it look old, and then shellac it to a stained piece of wood.

There were probably twelve cases in this inner sanctum, and I naturally started from the left side and slowly and deliberately looked at each scroll, admiring the "ancient words" that mean so much to the Christian faith. I had just finished one that contained pieces of II Chronicles and moved on. It was about at the fifth one that I read the gold plaque on the front of the case: "Habakkuk 2:1–10." I was stunned.

In my heart, I could hear the Lord saying to me: *Remember?* Instantly, I recalled myself as that lonely nine-year-old boy lying on my bed, uncovering this Scripture for the first time. All the feelings I had some thirty-four years earlier came pouring back, and I was suddenly caught between the two stages of my life. *You felt like such a loser the night I gave you this promise,* the Lord's voice continued. *Yesterday, at the tomb, you said on camera you had experienced one of the greatest moments in your life, and today, I'm reminding you again of this promise.*

At that moment, I realized God was tying together what seemed to be the painful, loose ends of my childhood with the present and future He had given me as an adult. And He was reminding me of the powerful words that had become the scripture for my life. He had whispered to me, a hurt little boy in Greenwood, Mississippi, what He had promised a prophet thousands of years ago: *Record a vision on your heart and hold it there, for though it may tarry, it will surely come.*

I trembled, and tears flowed down my cheeks as I realized that God was redeeming that promise to me. The irony of my being in Jerusalem in the first place flooded over me, and I smiled. We had been there to shoot a video for a song for the next summer's Vacation Bible School and, in fact, were leaving for home later that night. The VBS theme that thousands of children would learn? "Boomerang Express: It All Comes Back to Jesus." In that moment God was telling me, *My promise to you that day long ago has come full circle today . . . it all comes back to Me.*

I could barely see through the flood of tears as I walked outside to find Lynne. "I gotta tell you what the Lord just did. It is so sweet, so amazing."

"It's even cooler than that, Jeff," she replied after I told her.

"What do you mean?"

"Well, that part of the shrine is only open this year as part of a special celebration for Israel's sixtieth anniversary of becoming a nation. At the end of this year, they will lock that room up, and no one knows when it will be open again. Most likely, Jeff, you would not have had this opportunity again in your lifetime. This was the only year you could have come here and seen that case in that open room."

That day provided me with a message I share with kids all the time: That's how God loves us. He knows the intimate places of our hearts and how to touch them. He knows just what we need. I can't possibly count the number of times I have stood before kids over the years and shared with them that particular verse. God gives kids desires and ambitions and dreams because there is a purpose somewhere down the road for them.

Many kids grow up feeling like outcasts, like they never fit into "the mold," whatever that is. But I have spoken that scripture over them continuously since 1987 because it is a life verse for me . . . and because it's important to encourage kids to hold on.

So, just hold on. Maybe you don't feel valued right now, but you are. Life isn't measured by weight and bad haircuts. Your identity is not revealed on a playing field, in a classroom, or by a tax bracket. You are valued by the Creator who looks only at your heart, your potential, and the purpose for which He has called you. That's where your dreams are born, and one day, with His promise, "they will surely come."

CHAPTER 19

GREAT COMPANION

In 1971 David Houston pulled on the heartstrings of country music lovers all over the planet when he sang, "The hurtin' in them sad old songs . . . settled down in a poor boy's bones . . . and I vowed I'd someday sing and play . . . in Nashville." It was such a hit for Houston that it helped spawn one of the greatest Chamber of Commerce campaigns of all time, as billboards dotting the landscape throughout the south beckoned star-struck country music hopefuls with "All Roads Lead to Nashville." Today, some sixty years after the Grand Ole Opry made the Ryman Theater one of the most revered music venues in the world, Nashville has a firm grasp on its claim as Music City, USA, and as the country music capital of the world.

It can be argued that the city which doubles as the Tennessee state capital is also known for the number of local eating establishments that are completely unique to Nashville. One of my favorites is Midtown Noshville Authentic New York Delicatessen. It was established in 1996 by a group of local investors who traveled from coast to coast and gleaned components from all the places they visited to create a local deli that has become one of Nashville's most beloved eateries.

It prides itself on inviting guests to come in, leave all their cares at the door, and enjoy their experience. It is a great place to go and start the day with an irresistible breakfast menu that includes the deli's famous griddle cakes, or end the day with some Carnegie Cheesecake with friends.

To be sure, Noshville has succeeded in living up to its billing. It has a reputation not only for its food and fun, but also for giving back to the community through its philanthropic efforts for the Special Olympics of Tennessee, the League of the Hearing Impaired, and the Nashville Zoo.

They may never know it, but fifteen years after Managing General Partner Tom Loventhal and his team of investors realized their dream, they unwittingly paved the way for their restaurant to become a haven of comfort for me, all because a meticulously dressed, eighty-something Southern Belle woman wanted to buy me a Bloody Mary on my birthday.

IF EVER THERE WAS A ROMANCE WORTHY OF A COUNTRY SONG, IT WAS the one experienced by my mama, Elinor Ruth Pinion, and my daddy, Carl Lee Slaughter. It started when an eighteen-year-old Carl crashed the birthday party of fourteen-year-old Ruth in 1951 and ended some fifty-eight years later when she died on Christmas Day in 2009.

On that festive day Carl and his best buddy, Bookie Keenum, boldly invited themselves to the home of Elmer and Louise Pinion in Brazil, Mississippi, even though they didn't know a single person at the party, including young Ruth. Instead of being angry, the starry-eyed girl became quite infatuated with the most mature teenager in the house. It was a typical party for a typical group of young teenagers. There was cake and laughter and games, including spin the bottle. But back in 1951, rather than kissing, players took a walk together. When Mama spun the bottle, it stopped at the handsome, eighteen-year-old party crasher and, true to the rules, the two went for a walk.

They were gone for not a short amount of time, and when they finally returned, smiling ear to ear, Ruth's daddy whispered to her mother, "Well, Mama, Ruth's in love. Those two will never be apart again." And, sure enough, they were madly in love.

Four years later, Carl was about to leave for a tour of duty in Germany for the United States Army, and he couldn't bear the thought of "his girl" soon graduating from high school and losing her to someone else, so he came up with the idea to elope. On April 23, just weeks before she would join the Class of 1955 in a graduation ceremony, Ruth, unbeknownst to her parents, took Carl's hand in marriage. After one weekend together (Ruth had told her parents she was going to spend the weekend with Carl's sister, Margie), Carl shipped off to Germany, and his new bride returned to Lambert High School for classes on Monday.

Ruth had an older sister named Betty, who had eloped when she was sixteen and never finished high school, a fact not lost on their parents, who always seemed to bring it up. As Ruth was getting ready to leave for her graduation ceremony, her obviously proud mama and daddy made such a big deal of it, telling Betty, "See, you could have been like Ruth. She finished school," and went on to list all these things her sister had accomplished. After Ruth and her mama left, Betty couldn't hold it in any longer. "Daddy, Ruth hasn't done anything different than me. She's already married, too!" With her shocking declaration she produced her sister's marriage license as an exclamation point. And with that, my granddaddy sat down on his couch and refused to go to the graduation.

Still, he let Ruth live at home for the next year-and-a-half, until her beloved soldier returned from Germany. Nine months later, their first child was born. They named her Vickie. By the time eighteen more months passed, Carla was born. Nearly four years after that, my parents moved forty-five minutes away and settled in Greenwood, the area where they would spend the rest of their lives, and where I was born in 1965.

My mama was the perfect Proverbs 31 woman. She was a terrific homemaker who had an amazing knack for cooking, cleaning, and serving. She never thought twice about doing for others, even as she raised her own family, and the only times I remember her sitting down for any length of time was at Christmas, after the tree was decorated, or when my sisters and I would play the piano and sing for her. Still wearing her Sally Sunflower Grocery Store polyester smock, she would stare at the tree, or close her eyes and smile as she soaked in the music.

She loved to laugh and especially loved decorating for Christmas and Easter. When she finished putting up the lights and ornaments on the tree, she would sit really still and "ponder all these things in her heart," just like Mary did at the birth of Jesus. But even with that sweet spirit, my mama was particular about things. She kept a meticulous home and everything had its place—even crown molding.

I remember my daddy trying to hang crown molding in the kitchen one night. He had worked all day, and even though he was tired, he was willing to hang a few pieces just over the place where his fish aquarium sat on the top shelf of a not-so-sturdy TV stand.

As he worked, Mama would walk in every so often and inspect each piece very carefully. She never used a tape measure or a level to hang anything in the house. She had a talent for "eyeing" something, and it would be dead-on every time. It was a talent she taught each of her children, and to this day, everything in my own home has been placed throughout the same way.

For a while, every piece Daddy hung met with her approval, but finally one caught her eye. Mama tilted her head ever so slightly, then said, "That piece is off."

"That piece is not off," Daddy countered, without even looking at her from the ladder.

"Yeah, it is."

"It is not off."

The battle was on, and they bantered back and forth until she finally stood her ground. "Measure it." So, Daddy grabbed the level and, sure enough, it was one-eighth of an inch off. "I told you," she said.

Daddy grabbed the piece of molding off the wall, and it swung like a pendulum right into that ten-gallon aquarium, which went crashing into a million pieces on the floor, spilling water and fish all over the kitchen. We all took cover, because it was just a matter of time before Mama exploded. Daddy tiptoed through the mess and ran out the back door, because he knew it was time for him the leave the house for a while.

MAMA WAS LEGENDARY FOR HER ABILITY TO COOK, AND SHE COULD stretch out a food budget like nobody's business. She had learned at a young age the art of canning food because of her involvement in her high school's 4H club. In addition, she spent lots of time in the kitchen with her own mother, and she carried that thriftiness into her adult years as she raised her young family.

She not only was careful to can food for future meals; she also was frugal when it came to clothes. That prudence almost killed us one night. Part of Daddy's work consisted of pouring blacktop on highways, and he would often come home with his clothes covered in asphalt. In an attempt to preserve his work clothes for as long as possible, Mama decided one night to soak his clothes in gasoline before putting them in the washing machine. Our house was so small that the washing machine was in the corner of the dining room and the dryer had its place in the corner of the den. Daddy was eating supper at the table in the dining room, right next to the washing machine, when Mama opened the lid and a spark ignited his clothes and caused an explosion.

It could have been a scene right out of *I Love Lucy*. The blast knocked my daddy out of his chair and across the room, where he almost tumbled down the steps leading to my sisters' room. Mama was left standing in shock with soot on her face, singed hair and eyebrows, and what was left of her melted Sally Sunflower smock.

There are too many stories like this to tell, but rest assured . . . that small house witnessed a lot of memorable experiences. And even after my daddy died in 2003, despite the occasional piece of crown molding or minor catastrophe, Mama was still madly in love with him. And she often talked about being reunited in Heaven with the two greatest loves of her life—Jesus and Daddy—someday. I always reminded her not to be in a hurry—that I still wanted (and needed) her here for a while longer.

I WAS GETTING READY TO LEAD A SUNDAY MORNING WORSHIP SERVICE IN Boca Raton, Florida, one day in April 2009 when my phone rang. I saw my mother's number pop up, so I answered. She was crying hard, like a little girl, and struggled between sobs to tell me that her sister Betty had just died suddenly.

She and Betty talked nearly every single day, usually in the morning. Betty had been diagnosed with leukemia and had had some back surgery, so Mama wanted to check on her quickly before she left for church. Mama said that Betty didn't sound right, that she began to slur her words. Mama told her to put her husband Clayton on the phone, but before Mama could tell him what was going on, Betty passed out. She never regained consciousness and died at the hospital.

After I hung up with her, and the initial shock wore off, I remembered something that had happened the week prior to Betty's back surgery. I took Mama to see her, and we had such a great visit. But as we drove away and she was waving to us from her front porch, I remember thinking, *She's waving goodbye to us for the last time.*

When I returned home for the funeral, Mama said, "I want you to wear a suit for your Aunt Betty's service. Let's go to JC Penney, and I'll buy one for you."

On July 4, we had a big family reunion. That's what we do. That's how we've always dealt with tragedy and heartbreak. We draw great strength and comfort in just being together, so everybody met at Aunt Linda's in New Albany, Mississippi. And, like always, we sang, danced, told stories we've told a million times, and laughed like it was the first time we'd ever heard them!

At the end of the day, Mama gave me a kiss and a hug and got in her car to drive back home to Carrollton. When she pulled out of the driveway and turned one last time to wave to me, I got that same weird feeling I had with Aunt Betty just a few months before.

About three weeks later, I was going to be close to Carrollton, so I planned to spend a few days with Mama. Everything about that weekend seemed out of place. I don't know if I could ever explain it, but something was certainly out of sorts, like we were on the verge of something life-changing.

When I arrived for the weekend, she gave me what she always called a "happy." A happy was a little gift she gave for no particular reason. It was just a little something to . . . make you happy. When I walked into my room, there were a couple of "happys" wrapped and sitting on my bed. They were two coffee mugs from Miss Sippy's, a local sandwich shop with the best tomato soup and grilled cheese you've ever put in your mouth.

As I looked at them, that odd feeling resurfaced. Something in me knew I would treasure these mugs forever because they might be the last "happys" I would ever get from her. My heart started racing because my greatest fear was something happening to my mother. Daddy had been gone six years, and I had treasured my mom more than ever during that time.

Before I left for my next event, I took the trash to the bin that sits on the edge of the gravel road in front of her home. When I turned to walk back to the house, the Lord stopped me in my tracks. Again that strange feeling came over me, but this time it was different. *Take it all in. Savor this moment. It's all about the change*, I felt the Lord say.

On August 21, I flew to Vancouver for my twelfth year of Summer Youth Celebration. When we landed, I turned on my cell phone and saw a message from Vickie. Usually she doesn't call me when she knows I'm traveling, so I knew something was up. Vickie's message was that she was at the doctor with Mama getting some blood work done because Mama had looked a little orange the last few days, and it seemed to be getting worse.

The whole time I was in Vancouver, I waited for some kind of update. First, Mama was admitted to the hospital. Then I found out that her bilirubin levels were sky high. Bilirubin is the brownish yellow substance found in bile that is produced when the liver breaks down old red blood cells and is eliminated from the body. When the levels are high, the skin and the whites of your eyes may appear yellow. Most of the time it is caused by liver disease or a blockage of the bile duct that prevents bile from passing between the liver and the small intestine, which was the case with Mama. A normal bilirubin count is one. Hers was fifteen. They decided to take her from the Greenwood Hospital to Jackson's River Oaks Hospital to put a stint in the bile duct of her liver to open up a flow. From that point on, the updates were few and far between as doctors ran tests throughout the week to find out what was going on with her. The camp experience I had looked forward to was diminished because I felt so out of touch with my family; I did take some comfort in knowing that Mama was in good spirits following the procedure and felt much better.

All the while I was informing a friend I had in Vancouver, Dr. Henry Lew, about my mother's condition. Later in the week, he said to me, "Jeff, you need to go home."

I was almost too scared to ask the next question. "How serious do you think it is?"

"I can't say for sure. I don't want to make any judgments, but it doesn't sound good. You really need to go home."

I still had a week to go in British Columbia, and even though I was battling through layers of emotions, the Lord was beautifully blessing the worship times with the teenagers there. In my weakness, He was so strong! I was drained, and my heart was heavy because I sensed something bad was coming. Each night I felt like I was going to fall apart, but my band guys on the trip, Wes Durbin and Chris Jackson, were a total Godsend to me. They prayed with me and were doing all they could to help me get through that week. Every night Wes would drop by my room, sit down on my bed, and ask, "How you doing, Mista Slaughter?" He'd knock on my door every morning around 6:30 and ask the same question. To this day and forevermore, he'll never know what that meant to me.

In light of my conversation with Dr. Lew, I got my flight moved up two days. Chris and I flew from Vancouver to Detroit, and during our layover there, my Aunt Linda called to tell me, "Jeff, your mom's tests came back. It's cancer, and it's malignant."

I lost my breath, fell against the wall, and slid to the floor. Everyone around me was busy getting to their gates, or reading their newspapers, or making business calls, but my world had just stopped.

Please, Lord, not again. I can't do this again. Please Lord, no. . . .

Everything went into slow motion, and I barely remember anything on that flight back to Nashville. It was 11:00 p.m. Friday night when I pulled into my driveway and saw my friends Linda Forrest and Leanne Albrecht sitting on my porch swing. As I dragged myself up the front steps, they met me with bittersweet smiles and embraced me. They stayed for a while to encourage me and pray for me. The next morning Chris headed home to Alabama, and I left for Mississippi.

When Mama got the news on Friday, she wanted to go home for the weekend, and Dr. Poole relented as long as she promised to come back on Monday. I took her back to Jackson two days later so that she and the doctor could discuss the course of action.

My sister Carla met us at Dr. Poole's office, where he began to thoroughly explain what would happen next. His plan was to send Mama into surgery on Wednesday to see the extent of her cancer. There were three possible scenarios. The best news would be if there was a small tumor at the base of the bile duct. This would be easy to remove and resect. The second possibility was that he might have to do the Whipple Procedure, which was a treatment for pancreatic cancer. It was an eight- to nine-hour surgery with a very long and painful recovery. Patients facing this surgery were told there was a chance they might not make it out of the operating room.

The last scenario was the worst. This was if they found cancer that was beyond anything they could remove surgically. In this case, chemo and radiation could possibly extend life for a little while longer, but not much.

Now that we knew the possibilities, it was time to prepare for surgery. Mama and I went back to Carrollton to take care of some things and pack. We left for Carla's the next day. On the way, Mama started telling me where everything was: paperwork, bank accounts, and so on.

"I don't want to hear that," I told her. I wanted to scream because I felt like she thought this was it, and the last thing I wanted was for her to give up. "Mama, you're going to be okay." I was crying, yet she was steady and calm.

She looked at me and said, "Hon, you have to be ready for 'what if.' You've got to listen to me so you'll know what to do if I don't make it."

Deep down I knew she was right, but it didn't make it any easier. My heart was breaking, my head was swimming, and I barely remember driving to my sister's house.

That night, Carla, her husband Tony, and I anointed Mama's head with oil and prayed over her. After we prayed, Carla and I sat on the floor and layed our heads in her lap just like when we were kids and needed her comfort, even though she was the one who was sick. We sat there in silence for a while as she gently stroked our heads.

We had to be at the hospital early the next day. I held Mama's hand as we traveled through the quiet serenity of the morning. I remember thinking how badly I wanted to have faith for a miracle. "The Lord has got this, Mama. You're going to be okay; I know it." Those were some of the few words spoken between us.

In true "Ruth Slaughter style," my mother anticipated a lot of family members meeting us at the hospital, even though it was so far from home and so early in the morning. Of course, she had her little "reception basket" ready with all of our favorite things. As I've said before, it is a customary practice on Mama's side of the family that when tragedy strikes, we're there for each other. When my Mama's brothers Mike and Glenn died seven weeks apart, the whole family met at my grandparents' home every weekend, drawing strength from each other. We were together during Daddy's death, and Mallorie's. So, it was no surprise that my sisters and their kids, Aunts Delo and Linda, Aunt Carolyn (Mama's sister-in-law), and cousins Angie and Jennifer were all there, along with my friends Eva Horne and Nancy Demus. Nancy had driven seven hours through the night and was there waiting for us. At the end of the day, she drove right back to Nashville.

Dr. Poole came out to greet all of us before the operation, and told us, "If I come out after just a couple of hours, that means we were able to do the best-case scenario. If it's eight to nine hours, you know I've done the Whipple. If you see me coming back in about forty-five minutes, that means it was the worst case, and that there was nothing I could do."

Panic came over me when he repeated what he had said just two days before, and I prayed so hard that one of the first two possibilities would play out.

I thought I was going to be sick when I saw Dr. Poole walking down the hall forty-five minutes later. He was walking slowly and had a very sad look on his face. "I'm so sorry," he said. "She is eaten up, and the tumor is so massive. It's in the body of the pancreas, which is the reason it was so hard to diagnose, but the size of it is what caused the blockage of the liver duct." As the tears began to roll down my face, he hugged me. "I'm not God," he said, "but I would say she probably has three months."

My mind flashed back to that day when she waved to me at the family reunion. I ran outside and fell on my knees and started dry heaving. I begged the Lord, "I can't do this. Please don't take her!"

I was supposed to be attending a Vacation Bible School meeting that day. I called Lynne Norris, one of the editors on the VBS team who produced all the music videos, and when she answered, I could hardly get the words out. I was crying so hard as I tried to tell her what had transpired. "We're going to stop everything and pray for you right now," she said. Lynne knew my mama and was so heartbroken for me.

When I walked back into the hospital, I was able to see Mama after she left the recovery room. As they were wheeling her into her room, I walked up to her bed. She had this pitiful look on her face. "He told me I'm eat up and it's all over," she said weakly. I had no idea she already knew, and I couldn't utter a word. The ache in my heart was deeper and greater than anything I'd ever experienced.

For twenty-four hours after the doctor broke the news to us, I felt like I was in limbo and lying in the pit. I couldn't sense the presence of God at all. The next day, after Carla and I had slept on either side of a couch beside Mama's bed, I got up and looked in the mirror and wondered why I couldn't feel Him. Then I heard Him: *I'm down here with you. I know you're in the miry clay, and I'll lay down there with you until you're ready to get up. You haven't felt me or heard me, but I haven't left you. When you're ready, I promise I'll lift you up.*

When I had spoken to Lynne the day before, she told me the VBS team had come up with the next year's theme. The title was "Big Apple Adventure: Where Faith and Life Connect." The songs for it were due in mid-September, but in light of what was happening, my team decided I could have all the time I needed to write them. "By Faith" came to me while sitting next to Mama's hospital bed. I wrote the rest of the songs in her house, on the very piano where I had learned to play. Through the process, I began to realize that these songs were part of Mama's legacy and came from the very faith she taught me, Vickie, and Carla. When the songs were all completed, my VBS team allowed me the honor of dedicating "Big Apple Adventure" to my mama.

AND SO THE DAILY REGIMEN OF TAKING CARE OF HER BEGAN. I WOULD stay through the week and go back to Nashville while Carla came on the weekends. Mama's younger sisters, Linda and Delo, would come often for a few days. They were great at keeping her laughing by telling stories and reminiscing about their childhood.

The most difficult part of taking care of Mama was "doctoring" her incision. Every day, two times a day, we had to dress the wound, which was a very deep and wide cut. It just wouldn't heal, and about a month after the surgery, I wondered if it ever would. Nevertheless, I tried to remain upbeat as I told her, "Mama, we're just going to believe that your Christmas present this year from the Lord will be your incision getting well . . . that it will be completely healed on Christmas Day."

By the time Thanksgiving arrived, we hoped Mama would be able to uphold the tradition of coming to stay with me on the Saturday after, which she and Carla had started doing after Daddy passed. Mama and Carla's birthdays are December 4 and 5, and they enjoyed coming to Nashville to celebrate. But it didn't look like it was going to happen this year. Mama hadn't handled foods well at all since her surgery, and that morning she was feeling really weak and nauseous.

I walked into my bedroom, sat on the edge of my bed, and quietly asked God for a huge favor. "Lord, all I want for Christmas for the rest of my life is this week with her. I know it's time. You've already told me that. But I'm begging you for one more good week with her."

Thirty minutes went by, and I heard her stirring around in her bedroom. When I walked in, I was amazed to find her dressed, made up, and packed. She was ready to go! The twinkle in her eyes had returned, and so had her smile. "I just started feeling so much better! I think I can make the trip!"

So, we packed the car and headed to Nashville. We hadn't been on the road an hour when Mama sat up high in her seat. "Ya'll hungry? You want some chicken?" So we pulled up at Zaxby's Restaurant in Batesville, Mississippi. There she was able to eat her absolute favorite food—fried chicken tenders—without getting sick.

After that, we drove three hours into Jackson, Tennessee, and stopped at a Pilot Truck Stop. When we walked in the door Mama's eyes got real big. *Uh oh*, I thought.

"Mama, what's wrong?" I said. Carla and I both thought she might be having a stroke.

"Those weinies over there sho' look good."

"You want a hot dog?"

"Yes, I do. And put some mustard on it."

I've never been more excited to fix a hot dog—with mustard—in my life, and she ate every bite.

A couple of hours later, we finally made it to my house. It had really been a fun trip. Mama felt great and was "cuttin' up" the whole way. We'd hardly walked in the door when she asked, "Ya'll want to order pizza?" Carla and I exchanged comical looks of both shock and elation. So, we got us a Jett's Pizza, and later on we topped off the night with some eggnog the way Mama liked it, with "a little extra nog."

That week Mama, Carla, and I partied like rock stars. We had parties at the house almost every night, went out to fancy restaurants, and visited with friends.

My friend, Tania Stapps, gave her a haircut and a makeover and pampered her like she was a queen. All the people I was closest to in Nashville seemed to drop by that week to visit. There was a constant flow of friends coming by to meet my mother. One night we stayed up late singing together with friends and musicians, and before we realized it, it was one o'clock in the morning. The next day, December 4, was Mama's birthday, so I thought she might want to sleep in. But true to my mama's nature, she wasn't about to stay in bed. Instead, she helped me clean my house and get all my Christmas stuff out. We had plans back in Mississippi for her birthday, but she was adamant that we were not leaving my house until it was clean and the decorations were up.

Finally, en route to Carrollton, we made it back in time for her birthday party at the Oakland Catfish House. We continued the celebration the next day, as it was Carla's birthday, at an upscale restaurant in Greenwood called Giardina's. Mama was the star of the hour, as so many people came by to tell her how amazing she looked.

For the next few days, we continued this whirlwind of seeing friends and celebrating life. By the time I had to go back to Nashville on December 10, I truly wondered, *Lord, have you healed her?*

Once I was back in Nashville, though, Linda and Delo called to let me know that Mama had come down with what they suspected was pneumonia, and it had knocked her down pretty hard. I suddenly remembered Dr. Poole telling us at the hospital that Mama didn't have a lot of time left.

I thought about everything that had transpired over the last few months and laughed at the beautiful moments we had shared together during that week of "last hurrahs" that the Lord gave us. And I cried at the thought that we probably would never have even a day like that again. I was very grateful that God answered my prayer about giving us that last week together, and I am still overcome with joy at the memories I have of my mama's smile, the depth of her laughter, and the legacy of all the people she touched.

As I made my way back to her house on a rainy Sunday night, I hit a huge, eight-point buck, which damaged the whole front passenger side of my car. It became a four-point after I hit it, and I remember thinking that Daddy was probably looking down with pride at the fact that I'd finally killed a deer. Sitting there on the side of the cold, dark, rain-slicked road I was thinking, *Lord, what else?* Ken, my brother-in-law, came to the rescue, and when I finally got to Mama's and saw how much she had gone down in just a few days, my heart sank at the realization of the inevitable.

ONE OF THE THINGS MY MOTHER LOVED ABOUT MY DOING THE VBS music was watching the DVDs we made. She got a tremendous joy out of watching her boy do something that pointed people to the Lord, because her whole life was dedicated to that legacy. Every year she looked forward to watching the newest VBS videos with me.

The DVD for "Saddle Ridge Ranch" had just come out, which we shot at the C U Lazy Ranch in Granby, Colorado. The C U Lazy is located where the Colorado River runs off the Continental Divide and winds its way through mountain valleys. When I was there in the previous spring, I had been taken in by the hundreds of acres of lush, green meadows, the vibrant, blue skies and the clean, crisp air. It was a perfect setting for the DVD, and I was excited to play it for Mama.

She was sitting in her recliner with a blanket over her. For really the first time since her diagnosis, I thought about how frail she now looked.

We watched "Who He Says I Am" and "What I'm Gonna Do." But after "Tumbleweed," she said, "Ohhh, that's the one they're going to love," and she smiled.

"Yeah, I think so, too," I said. Then I played "God Cares." For some reason, I had cried all through that shoot. Maybe it was the beauty of the Colorado Rockies behind me, but I was just completely overcome with emotion the whole time we were filming that song.

Now, seven months later, as Mama and I watched the video, she suddenly said, "Who are all those beautiful women around you?"

"What are you talking about, Mama? There aren't any women around me."

"Yes. They are there, Jeff. They are all around you, and they are singing and worshipping and doing the motions with you."

I didn't know what to say. She wasn't on any medication, so it was obvious she wasn't hallucinating or seeing things that weren't there. All of a sudden I heard the Lord say, *She's seeing angels . . . she's in between two worlds, and she can see things you can't now. That's what you were feeling that day in Colorado. Your spirit was feeling my angels all around you, but your flesh couldn't see it. They were preparing you for this.*

When "Like Jesus" came on the screen, Mama said, "Oh my goodness! That is the most beautiful table of food I have ever seen. How in the world did ya'll get that table out there like that?" I felt the Lord say, *She's seeing My table because she is about to sit down there, and that is the place where you finally become like Me.*

On December 15, the senior citizens group at North Greenwood called the LLL (Live Long and Love It) were having their Christmas party, and Mama was determined to go. She got up and got ready that morning and looked so beautiful. A woman who never missed a Sunday, she had not been able to go to church since her diagnosis, so she was excited to see everyone. I realize now she went to say goodbye. We stopped at the doctor's office right afterward to do some blood work, and they immediately admitted her to the hospital because of her pneumonia.

In the days following, she plummeted. Once she got in the hospital bed, she never ate another bite of food, and she slept almost constantly, except at night, when she would struggle to breathe. I would get up, open the window, and fan her face with a paper plate to give her some relief. I don't remember getting much sleep during those days. It was a hard, hard week. On Friday, Dr. Doug Bowden, a surgeon and dear family friend who was a member of our church, stopped by to check on her. We were in the bathroom when he came in.

"Doug, I want to go home," Mama said.

"Well, I'd like to run some scans of your abdomen."

"Why?"

"What is it, Doug?" I asked.

He spoke calmly and gently. "Well, I feel that the tumor has gotten so large that it may have shut off the entrance to the stomach."

So I asked, "If that's the case, what can we do?"

A tear formed in his eyes and he couldn't say anything.

I was amazed at how calm my mother was. And I remember thinking, *It's over.*

"Like I said, Doug," she repeated. "It's time for me to go home. Jeff, pack up my things."

By the time I got to the car with the first load, I was crying so hard that I was almost doubled over and could barely open the trunk. A woman walked by. She had long, sandy blonde hair and was wearing a floral print dress that flowed in the cold, December breeze.

Her smile was sweet and comforting. "Looks like someone is getting ready to go home."

"Yes, they are."

She never reacted to my sobbing. She just smiled and walked on.

Our drive through town was quiet and reflective. There were the memories of Christmas parades, and Shipley's Donut Shop. There was Chaney's Court Square, a pharmacy where we would buy bubblegum for a penny and get our pictures made. We ate at the Crystal Grill and shopped at JC Penney's, and loved to go up those big stairs to visit Santa Claus. Everything about that town was like Mayberry.

We passed by Presbyterian Day School where I had attended for a few of my elementary years. "I remember standing on that sidewalk waiting for you to pick me up, and the best sight to me all day was when your car pulled around the corner," I said to my mother.

She smiled.

"Mama, I can't give up on you. No matter what any doctor says, I can't give up on you, and I don't want you to give up, either."

"Jeff, honey, I'm not giving up. I'm just ready to go."

When we arrived at Mama's house, Carla drove up behind us. We couldn't have timed it more perfectly. Something had told her to leave work early in Jackson and come on down. She was stunned at how much Mama had declined in a week.

The next morning I drove to Nashville to quickly take care of some things and pack more clothes. When I opened my suitcase I felt the Lord say, *Take your suit.*

I slowly walked into my closet, where I had hung the suit Mama bought me to wear for my Aunt Betty's funeral. As I carefully laid it on the bed, my knees buckled, and I hit the floor. Sobbing, I screamed, "Lord, this is the hardest thing I've ever had to do, and I don't know how to do it. You've got to help me!"

In a mental fog, I drove back to Carrollton the next morning. When I got to Mama's, the house was full of people. It was like somebody had already died. We made the call to hospice, and Thomas came out that afternoon. We took him into the kitchen and started signing forms, and he pulled out the morphine pack, which is used to help alleviate pain, but can depress respirations. When I saw it, I panicked because I was the one who had administered it to Daddy, and though I know it eased his pain and didn't actually cause his death, I still carried a heavy guilt for giving it to him. "I can't do it! I can't do it again!"

Carla said, "I'll do it, Jeff. You had to do it for Daddy; I'll do it for Mama."

Then my cousin Tammye, who is a nurse and who dropped everything to come be with us when Mallorie died, said, "No, I'll do it." So, from that Sunday night until Christmas Eve, she took amazing care of Mama. Throughout that week she kept a journal of every time she gave her medication, every visitor that came by, every conversation that took place in the room, and even every time Mama opened her eyes.

On Wednesday my cousin Angie told me she had to go to Memphis, which is a two-hour drive north of Carrollton. "Do you need me to get something for your Mama?" She asked it very gently, and I knew exactly what she meant. She was asking me if I needed her to get Mama an outfit.

"Yes," I told her. "And it needs to be red and it needs to be royal. I don't care what it costs." All my life I had heard my mother say, "You know, your Daddy just loves me in red."

Angie came back with a beautiful, rich red long-sleeved blouse and black velvet skirt. The blouse had very elegant ruffles around the collar and cuffs, and the buttons were works of art. It was one of the most beautiful outfits I have ever seen, and certainly worthy of my mother.

Tammye left so that she could be with her husband, Donnie, and their two children for Christmas Eve. Carla administered the morphine for Mama as I was reading Psalm 40 over her: "I waited patiently for the Lord; He turned to me and heard my cry. He lifted me out of the slimy pit, out of the mud and mire. . . ." She smiled, ever so slightly. "He set my feet on the rock and gave me a firm place to stand. . . ." Weakly, she raised her hand as if in worship. And when I read, "He put a . . ." she whispered "neeew sooong," and that was all she could say. I couldn't say anything else, either.

Later on, I heard the clock chime at midnight, so I quietly walked back to Mama's room and went to her bedside. "Mama, it's Christmas." She opened her eyes and smiled. "Merry Christmas."

I told her how much I loved her and what she meant to me and how honored I was to have been her son. I told her how proud I was of her and how I had watched her consistently live out her faith her whole life. "I don't know how you could have loved me better or taught me more about trusting the Lord."

On Christmas morning I went in the bathroom feeling crushed to the point that I couldn't bear it any longer. I could hear my mother in her bed next door, and she was strangling just like my daddy did. I begged, *Lord, you can stop this. Please stop this.*

Then I felt Him say, *Yes, I could have come off the cross too . . . but I didn't do that either.*

So I shut my mouth.

But He did give me two more special moments with Mama. The first one was like something out of *Steel Magnolias*. Just before she died, she looked up beyond us and smiled and said, "Daddy!" She had always called my father that.

"Mama, do you see Daddy?" I asked.

"Yes. He's right there."

Vickie asked her, "Mama, do you see Mallorie?"

"Yes, she's standing there holding your daddy's hand."

Delo chimed in. "Ruth, do you see Mother and Daddy?"

"Yes."

Linda asked about their brothers next. "What about Mike and Glenn. Are they there?"

"Yes. I see them. They're right there."

It was such a joyful and sweet moment.

Then Linda asked about their older sister in her sweet Southern Belle tone, "Ruuuth, do you see Betty?"

A pause. "No."

Linda and Delo let out a simultaneous gasp, and their eyes got big as saucers. "Ohmigosh, she doesn't see Betty! She doesn't see Betty!"

"Give me a break. She's up there." I said. Then we all couldn't help but laugh. Even at a moment like this and not even realizing it, Mama was making us smile when we were hurting so bad.

A moment later, the Home Health nurse, Amanda, checked Mama's pulse, and I heard Amanda say, "She's gone."

I was leaning right over Mama, and as the light came through the window and shone on her face, it instantly relaxed. The crease in her forehead that she always hated suddenly disappeared. Growing up, my sisters and I had watched her put lotion on that crease and rub it to try and make it go away. The moment her suffering ended, that crease instantly disappeared, and she seemed to look thirty years younger. Her beautiful face was relaxed, her natural coloring had returned, and she was now free from the excruciating pain she had suffered for the last four months. And I felt the Lord say, *I let you see her the moment she saw Me.*

Indeed, God did heal her on Christmas Day, just like I had told her so many times.

ON THE DAY BEFORE HER FUNERAL, MY SISTERS AND I WERE LAUGHING about how Mama had told me that we had better make sure she looked good and we'd better not let the old men at the morgue do her hair and makeup. "If you do," she said in as serious a tone as she could muster, "I'll come back and get every one of ya'll."

So when we got there, Mama's hair was wet and slicked back, and the room was white and sterile and had that smell of formaldehyde. I had been fixing her hair for the last couple of months because she didn't have the strength. I had brought the flat iron I'd been using to curl her hair. When I turned the first section of hair around the iron, it flipped back straight again, and some of it came out. "Oh, my gosh!" I gasped. "Her hair is coming out!" In the meantime, Linda and Delo were working on her makeup. "Boooyyy, you better not mess it up," Delo warned. Thank goodness I managed the rest without any more problems.

Vickie's son Jay preached Mama's service the next day. The aunts and the cousins honored Mama's life by gathering around the piano—like we had done so many times throughout the years—and sang a medley of Mama's favorites such as "Blessed Assurance," "Great Is Thy Faithfulness," and "What a Day That Will Be." I sang "Beulah Land," just as I had at my grandmother's funeral years before. To top off the emotional day, I was touched by the fact that eighteen of my friends came down from Nashville, most of whom drove five hours, attended the funeral, and turned around to drive right back home.

January 10 is my birthday, and for the first time in my life, I was dreading it. For forty-four years my mama had sung "Happy Birthday" to me at 6:30 in the morning.

My friend Kristine Stroupe, whose own mother was battling pancreatic cancer, sent me a Facebook message on the sixth. "I was praying for you, and Papa said that you are really sad about your birthday this year. And He said for me to tell you that He has an incomprehensible gift for you. He didn't tell me what it was. He just said you would know it when you received it."

The night before my birthday, I went to bed with a heavy, heavy heart. But sometime during the night I had a vision of my mother just like she looked when I was a little boy. Her hair was jet black, and she was beautiful. She walked into my room, bent down to kiss me, and said, "I love you, boy. Happy birthday." When I woke up, there was this peace, this sweetness that filled the room, and I just knew she'd been there. Lord, the veil between our two worlds is really . . . so . . . thin.

I was glad to see that Linda Gross was working when I met my friend, Linda Forrest, at Midtown Noshville for breakfast. Linda has worked at Noshville since it opened, and nobody loves the people she serves more than she does. She had just beaten cancer herself through her faith and determination. That morning while we were celebrating Linda's life and my birthday, I noticed an elderly and meticulously dressed woman sit down at the other side of the bar. Linda Gross went over to talk to her and when she came back, she said, "Jeff, I know you're here before church, but this lady wants to buy you a Bloody Mary for breakfast."

I didn't know what to say, but I didn't want to insult her, either. "You know what, Linda, if she wants to bless me like that, then bring it on."

When I had finished my meal and was waiting for the check, Linda Gross came over and said, "She wants to pay for your breakfast, too."

I got up and walked over to this precious woman who had blessed me so much. She seemed to have all the characteristics of my mama. She was obviously feisty, very particular about her appearance, and loving, with a very generous heart.

"You are so sweet," I told her. "You started my day off just right. What is your name?"

"Ruth."

Tears welled up in my eyes, and I took a deep breath. "That was my mother's name. It means 'Great Companion.'" I could see a tear roll down her cheek. There were several rolling down mine as well. "Thank you for being so sweet to me. It was like having my mother buy me breakfast today."

Kristine was right. His gift was, indeed, incomprehensible.

CHAPTER 20

IDENTITY CRISIS

Iᴅᴇɴᴛɪᴛʏ ᴄᴀɴ ʙᴇ ᴀ ꜰʀᴀɢɪʟᴇ ᴛʜɪɴɢ. Wʜᴇɴ ɪᴛ ɪꜱ ᴄʜᴀɴɢᴇᴅ ᴏʀ ᴛᴀᴋᴇɴ away, it can be devastating. When my mama died on Christmas Day of 2009, it meant that my identity as a son was gone, because I was nobody's "little boy" anymore. I didn't have a parent to lean on or gain advice from when I needed it. And I really needed it when I thought I had lost my identity as a writer of children's music.

For sixteen years, most of my identity was wrapped up in LifeWay. Between 1997 and 2012 I had been the writer of all Vacation Bible School songs, and the face on the DVDs that taught churches and children the motions to those songs. Over the years, more than 46 million people worldwide had sung those songs. Our videos had gone triple platinum and sold more than 150,000 copies.

But in January 2010 I began to feel a shift in my relationship with LifeWay, just weeks following my mother's death. LifeWay revealed a new direction in the way the VBS leadership wanted the music written and produced, starting with their replacement of a Grammy Award–winning producer I had closely worked with for eleven years. I was willing to go along with this, but a feeling began to grow within me that maybe God was leading me in a new direction as well.

Despite the change and working with a new producer, I felt we put out a strong product in "Big Apple Adventure." When it came time to write and produce the music for 2012's "Amazing Wonders Aviation," LifeWay didn't really have a producer in mind, so I suggested Preston and Spencer Dalton, two very talented brothers with whom I was already working on another project. The Daltons are a super anointed, creative team, and I felt they could help me take the VBS music production to a new level.

After "Aviation" was completed, there were concerns about mixing and production. This eventually led to a meeting with me and leaders from the VBS and the music departments in August 2011 to discuss VBS 2013 and beyond. A few weeks prior, when I was filming the promo video for "Aviation" in Van Ness Auditorium, I was waiting for the video team to get started when I saw this vision in my mind of a huge group of people celebrating all the years of videos I had shot. I immediately thought, *Lord, am I going to die? Are they going to have some kind of memorial in here for me?* At that time I had no idea I was going to walk away from LifeWay.

The Lord began to speak to me about events that were about to transpire over the next few months. He literally went down a checklist of what was going to happen . . . and every single thing eventually did happen just as He had said.

At first, I was afraid of the thought of walking away. After all, I had always said that I would write VBS music for LifeWay until I went to a retirement home. Besides, after investing sixteen years of my life with them there had been little room for the Lord to put anything else in my hands. But, once I let go, there was room for God to put there what He wanted, and He brought me total peace.

So, finally on November 1, 2011, during a conference call with some members from the VBS and music departments, I decided to bow out graciously. And despite the difficulty of walking away, God poured grace over me, and I didn't shed a tear. I heard God tell me to jump out into the great unknown, and that's what I did because He reminded me of His promise: *I've never let you down in forty-six years, so don't worry.*

In the end, I felt like sixteen years had been a great run. I have come to appreciate the Biblical significance of numbers. The number sixteen represents achievement. It took sixteen years for the four Gospels to be completed. I felt the Lord saying, *For sixteen years you have written My Gospel through music, and that's a wonderful achievement. I am proud of you. Sixteen is also a number of coming of age,* He continued. *So be encouraged that there is so much more. You've achieved a lot in the past, but I want to show you more.*

Even though I was at peace with my decision, the Enemy was pressing in on me. Many mornings I woke up with a tightness in my chest and a shortness of breath. And then the "what ifs" would come. *What if I lose my house? What if there are no more opportunities to write? What if the only question I ask every day is "would you like fries with that?"* I realized that while I was spiritually walking the path with God, up to that point I had been coasting. It's easy to live life when things are going well. I began freaking out because I didn't know what was going to happen. To top it all off, because of some mix-up with my royalties, all of a sudden there was no money coming in.

I knew I needed to press into the Lord as hard as I could. I committed to getting up early every morning to spend time with Him. Before all this had started, my time with God had become sporadic because of my crazy travel schedule and the general busyness of writing and performing. There had been no real consistency in my time with the Lord. But now I knew nothing else was going to sustain me except His presence, and I had to seek it with everything that was within me. I began to crave my time with Him, and it didn't matter how early I had to get out of bed to do it.

In His mercy and tenderness, God kept reminding me, *In this season you're going to have to trust me. You have to walk by faith. You have to do all these things you've been writing about for so many years. All those lyrics you've written in the past . . . do you really believe them?* Out of all the hundreds of songs I had written over the years, the one line the Lord kept bringing back to me was, "I will not worry, I will not be afraid," from the song "God Cares." As the days passed, He began to confirm in me more and more that no matter how mysterious the future was to me, He was on this journey with me. He was leading it, in fact, and we were in the right place.

I had a devotion book titled *Jesus Calling* by Sarah Young, and the writing for November 1 was this:

Do not be discouraged by the difficulty of keeping your focus on Me. I know that your heart's desire is to be aware of My Presence continually. This is a lofty goal; you aim toward it but never fully achieve it in this life. Don't let feelings of failure weigh you down. Instead, try to see yourself as I see you. First of all, I am delighted by your deep desire to walk closely with Me through your life. I am pleased each time you initiate communication with Me. In addition, I notice the progress you have made since you first resolved to

live in My Presence. When you realize that your mind has wan-
dered away from Me, don't be alarmed or surprised. You live in a
world that has been rigged to distract you. Each time you plow your
way through the massive distractions to communicate with Me, you
achieve a victory. Rejoice in these tiny triumphs, and they will in-
creasingly light up your days.

A friend had given me this book on my birthday in 2009. When Mama got sick in August, we tried to do devotionals every day, so we began to read it together. After she died, I couldn't bring myself to pick it up again. But on this cold day in November, when the most important conference call of my life was just hours away, it provided me the courage to do what I knew the Lord was calling me to do: Walk away.

At 6:30 a.m. on December 1, I woke up to my phone buzzing and vibrating. Messages started pouring in from people wondering what had happened because they'd already seen LifeWay's announcement about my departure. I had no idea they would release it before January. But when I got up and checked out the LifeWay website, sure enough, there it was.

I remember the Enemy attacking my heart again with panic and fear because now everyone knew and there was no turning back. But I also knew that neither fear nor doubt come from the Lord, so when I felt an attack coming on, I went to my couch to pray and read the Word.

All the while, I had people speaking blessings over me and praying for me. One email I received that I will never forget came from a friend in Oklahoma: "Jeff, this may be the end of an era, but it's not the end of a destiny." In the middle of such chaos, I began to feel this intense sense of peace come over me. The Lord kept reminding me that people were praying for me: *You've been battling a spirit akin to the prince of Persia who was attacking Daniel—and it was an intense battle—but through the prayers of your Christian brothers and sisters, peace has broken through.*

The reference from the Lord was from Daniel 10. Daniel had been praying for three weeks for a breakthrough, but his prayers were hindered by Satan's forces. God used Michael the archangel to break the barrier, and Daniel's prayers were heard and answered. And because of Daniel's persistence, he found favor with the Lord. In my case, God was honoring the prayers of so many Christian friends, brothers and sisters in the Lord, some of whom I didn't even know. Their humble and persistent prayers on my behalf brought peace and strength to my weakened spirit. As I stood in my bathroom, looking in the mirror, I felt God was helping me turn a corner.

This happened on the morning of December 2—Mallorie's birthday—and my reading from *Jesus Calling* helped mirror that breakthrough of peace. It read, "I am the Prince of Peace. . . . My peace is steadfastly with you. When you keep your focus on Me, you experience both My Presence and My Peace." Next, I picked up my One Year Bible, and the Old Testament reading for that day was Daniel 9:1–11:1, which includes the whole story of the Prince of Persia and Michael the archangel.

When I told my agent, Dena DiVito, about the connection of my two readings, she almost whispered, "Jeff, last night my whole devotion before bed was about Michael the archangel battling through the Prince of Persia to get to Daniel and protect him." Dena also told me that when she told her mother about my situation, her mom started to cry, and said that she had felt the Lord specifically tell her to begin praying for me and she didn't know why. "Then she got up and turned on her television to watch a preacher she enjoyed listening to, and his whole message was about Daniel and the Prince of Persia," Dena said.

I began to pray to the Lord to help me to find a new career path specifically on December 8, 2011. Twelve is the number of establishment (the twelve tribes of Judah established government); eight is the number of new beginnings (the eighth day is the beginning of a new week); and eleven is the number of revelation, because Joseph was the eleventh son of Jacob and he was the revealer of dreams.

So, I thought it would be cool for my "new beginning" to start on that day. Little did I know, but on that day, my friend Johnathan Crumpton had left a message on my phone. I hadn't heard from him in sixteen years, so I didn't recognize his number. When I retrieved the message, I heard his voice say, "Bro, I heard that you left LifeWay, and we need to talk. When can we grab lunch?" Johnathan is the vice president of Brentwood Benson Music Publications, which owns close to 60,000 copyrights, making it the world's largest catalog of Christian music publishing.

As soon as I heard his voice, I knew what he was thinking.

I called him back, and we set up a meeting for December 16. Dena, her assistant Eric Wright, and I met with Johnathan for lunch. The first thing he told me was that he had spoken to Dale Matthews, then the president of Brentwood Benson, and they wanted to create a "Jeff Slaughter" brand of music for kids, including VBS and other music products. And that brought up the one thing that helped me see a light flicker once again. "Jeff, we certainly want you to do a ton of things with us, but the most pressing project right now is our kids' Christmas musical, and we want you to do it," Johnathan said. "We should have already started it, but I kept feeling the Lord tell me to hold off. Now I know why. You're supposed to write it. We just established a partnership with Soles4Souls, and we want their mission to be the central focus of this musical."

I could hardly contain myself, because Soles4Souls was an organization that was dear to me. It was a project born of great need and great compassion by Wayne Elsey following the Asian tsunami disaster in December 2004. Elsey, like many around the world, was sitting at home watching television coverage of the tsunami, when a camera shot of one lone shoe washing up on the beach compelled him to do something. With a few calls to footwear executives, 250,000 shoes were donated. A few months later, when Hurricane Katrina ravaged the Gulf Coast, Elsey again solicited donations, and more than 1 million pairs of shoes were sent to those in need. After that, Elsey established the nonprofit Soles4Souls, and today millions upon millions of pairs of shoes are donated and sent around the world.

Dena and I had been trying on our own to establish something with Soles4Souls as well, but it hadn't happened. It now became very clear to me that God's work in this was huge. God was providing the very opportunity I had been seeking. I sensed Him saying to me, *Go where I'm opening doors. If I'm not opening that door, don't even worry about it. Let it go. I opened the door to Brentwood Benson right off the bat; that's where I'm leading you. Go there.*

The result from that meeting has been a partnership with a company that believes in me and my heart for children and in the power of changing the world through global missions.

By January 2012, I was working on a children's Christmas musical called *The Christmas Shoe Tree*, which was arranged by the talented Dalton brothers. At the same time, Brentwood Benson asked me to create its inaugural 2013 Vacation Bible School. So, we began work on the "Jeff

Slaughter VBS World Tour," which would be released in the fall. Over the next six months, I was consumed by God's grace and provision as He guided us in both endeavors.

Remember the vision I described earlier that I had while sitting in the Van Ness auditorium at LifeWay? Well, in January 2012, I was leading my last VBS Institutes and Previews for "Amazing Wonders Aviation." I had no idea that my beloved VBS team had put together a beautiful farewell celebration for me to take place during these conferences. The first one was at Ridgecrest. As the tribute came to a close, Jerry Wooley, a VBS specialist, announced that LifeWay had put together a video of snippets from all the videos I had filmed through the years. When it was over, the crowd rose to their feet in celebration! As soon as the video started, I began to weep, realizing that this truly was the Lord's plan all along and that He had revealed this exact moment to me seven months earlier. And, of course, as you probably remember by now, seven is the number of completion.

In June, *The Christmas Shoe Tree* was released, and by the fall children's choirs all over the United States were engaged in an effort to change the world, one shoe and one soul at a time. Our hope was that through this musical, we could educate, challenge, and inspire kids, churches, and communities to come together in a unique and powerful way to make a difference. By God's grace and through His blessing, *The Christmas Shoe Tree* was received so well that it became the top-selling children's Christmas musical in the country.

In the process, God was teaching me to trust Him, and He was continually reinforcing His faithfulness to the calling He had given me. My identity truly was found in Him, and my purpose was to live out the plan He had placed for me on the other side of open doors.

CHAPTER 21

CAN'T STOP THESE SHOES

God's Word says we should *walk with* Him. Jesus asked His disciples to *follow* Him. Most of us are familiar with Romans 10:15: "How beautiful are the feet of those who bring good news!" Jesus washed the disciples' *feet*; Mary sat at Jesus' *feet*; God's Word is a lamp unto our *feet*; and He keeps our *feet* from stumbling on the path. There's a definitive pattern in the Bible that teaches us the importance of using our feet.

I began to focus on many of these scriptures after I had written the song "By Faith" for the "Big Apple Adventure" VBS and was in New York City in August 2010 preparing to shoot one of the music videos. The biggest theme of that song is declaring that no matter what happens in life, we must choose to walk by faith. My good friend Jeff Arnold, who was the producer and director for that project, decided that because we were going to focus on "walking by faith," I needed some shoes that would make my feet really "pop."

The night before we were to begin filming, we passed a store and saw a pair of yellow and red Onitsuka Tiger athletic shoes sitting in the display window. "There they are!" Jeff declared, as if he'd just found a winning lottery ticket. "You gotta wear those shoes. I don't care what they cost. You're buyin' 'em!"

That moment spawned a ministry and a lifestyle that I could never have imagined. Once the video was released to the public, I started receiving tons of comments about those yellow and red shoes on my website, and it's been fun sharing the story of how the Lord birthed the whole idea. Every time I wear those shoes, it's a great reminder for me to stay focused on what my feet are doing. I know I want them to keep moving and doing what God made me to do. I know I want to follow the path of His incredible plans and purposes and to never stray from walking in His ways.

But I had no idea they'd take me to the other side of the world.

A FEW WEEKS AFTER FILMING THE "BY FAITH" VIDEO, I WAS WALKING OUT of the Frothy Monkey, a Nashville coffee shop near my home, when I met Amanda Lawrence, who was then the executive director for an organization called Visiting Orphans. She was meeting with Jeff Arnold to discuss a project they were working on together. Five minutes into our conversation, she said, "You've got to go to Uganda with us in March."

"Okay." The word came out of my mouth before I realized it.

I would be traveling to Uganda with a team of about twelve people who had all been working to raise support to cover the cost of the trip. Churches and friends had committed enough money to the mission that there was a large surplus left over. With that extra money, the team was able to buy 160 pairs of shoes and a brand-new loom for making fabric for one orphanage. We had set aside a day to wash the kids' feet and put the new shoes on them. When we told the kids at the orphanage that they were getting new shoes, you'd have thought they were getting a million dollars. They squealed and laughed and jumped up and down. The shoes were simple ones that they could wear with their daily uniforms, but they might as well have been Uggs and Sperrys.

Even though I was now forty-six years old, I realized that I had never washed anyone's feet in an act of humility and service, like Jesus did for His disciples. But after we washed the feet of those precious children, I understood why the Lord encouraged us to do that in His Word. This was a pivotal moment in my life and in my heart. As I watched the kids admiring their new shoes, I remember thinking that every time they put them on their feet, they'd be reminded of this day and of the group of people who cared for them. Most important, they would remember that we told them about Jesus and how very much He loves them.

Canaan Children's Home was a three-hour drive from the airport, and my first night in Uganda was a real eye-opener. I quickly found my driver who, along with two of his friends, would be taking me to the orphanage. They couldn't quite comprehend my efforts at doing the "Mississippi thing," that is, trying to carry on a "long-lost buddy" type of conversation with them right off the bat. When it became obvious that all efforts at communicating were completely lost in translation, I decided to take a nap. Three times I woke up to find us stopped at various checkpoints in the bush with military men carrying uzis and staring coldly at each of us. I suddenly realized at that moment that no one in my life knew where I was. I could disappear very easily, and not a soul would have a clue where to find me. It was a sobering thought, until I also realized, *Well, there's nothing I can do about it now.* So I went back to sleep.

We arrived after midnight, and Mama Rebecca, the wife of Pastor Isaac, the orphanage's director, brought me some food before sending me off to the barracks that would serve as my home for the next week. After sleeping for about six hours, I woke up to the sound of children playing outside in an open-air pavilion where they ate their meals and conducted their Bible studies. I basically rolled out of bed and decided to walk out to say hello, when I found out I was about to lead the kids in a time of worship. Diana Perkey, one of the members of our team, was going to lead a Bible study for the kids after worship. She and Stephanie Moon, another member, were going to help me with music. I hadn't even had a cup of coffee yet.

I had thought about certain songs I wanted to teach the kids on the first day. I began with "Who He Says I Am." I wanted to teach them a song that talked about who the Lord says they are, and that told them even if they had no earthly family, they still had a Daddy who loves them very much. We started with the verse, "He says I am made in His image; He says I am one of His children. . . ."

There was no keyboard to be found, so it was a little difficult at first. All of a sudden, one of the boys grabbed an African drum and started goin' at it! He could have given a lot of drummers in Nashville a run for their money. Suddenly the song took on a whole new sound. When all the beautiful voices blended with the drum, this "American" song was transformed into an authentic African melody.

Early the next morning I woke to the sounds of Muslims in the distance chanting their first prayers of the day. As I lay there, looking up at the mosquito netting that surrounded my bed, I noticed the first rays of sunlight begin to creep across the horizon. I could also hear that some of the boys were already up and playing outside. Then I began to hear a sweet little voice sing, "He says I am made in His image; He says I am one of His children. . . ."

It may have been the most beautiful thing I'd ever heard, because it was so innocent, so genuine, and so pure. This little boy was beginning to understand that the void left behind by parents, who were no longer living, could be filled by the One Who created him. In that moment, tears began to roll slowly down my face, and I felt the Lord say, *I gave you that song for him. You wrote it for VBS, but I brought you to the other side of the world to teach it to him.*

I FIRST MET ROB AND JULIE NEAL IN 1991, WHEN ROB EXTENDED THE opportunity for me to take his position as keyboardist for the Christian band GLAD. He and his wife wanted to move back to Springfield, Missouri, so after someone recommended me for that position, he gave me a call. However, when he mentioned that I'd have to move to West Virginia, I quickly yet very politely declined. Then, over the next three hours we built a bond of friendship that has lasted more than twenty years.

In September 2010 I was visiting Rob and Julie while I was in Springfield playing an event. "I think I'm supposed to go to Ethiopia with you next year," I had told Julie.

"Well, let's pray about it and see what the Lord works out," she replied with a smile. The Neals had adopted two little boys from neighboring villages in Ethiopia. During the adoption process, Rob and Julie visited these villages often, only to discover that the search for clean water was an everyday struggle. With little drinkable water, disease was rampant. Julie felt the tug of the Lord leading her to raise money needed to build wells in each of these villages.

In April 2011, after my return from Uganda, Amanda Lawrence and her husband Simon asked me to travel back to Africa in August, this time to join them as an artist partner in Ethiopia. They explained that as an artist partner with Visiting Orphans, "You'll do what you normally do leading VBS songs for the kids, and we'll cover your expenses for the cost of the trip," Amanda said. "There is this couple in Springfield, Missouri, who have been raising money to build two water wells there, and we think you'd be a perfect fit to go and lead worship with all the kids."

I couldn't believe what I was hearing. "Are you talking about Rob and Julie Neal?"

Amanda's eyes popped wide open. "Do you know them?"

"Wait a minute. You're telling me that you'll pay my way to go to Ethiopia in August with Rob and Julie Neal to check out the water wells they're having built? Hold on." I picked up my phone, called Rob, and said, "Bro, I'll see you in August! You're not gonna believe this!"

Once we got to Ethiopia a few months later, I immediately began to compare it with my earlier trip to Africa. I had thought Uganda was third world . . . until I got to Ethiopia. Sadly, this was on a whole other level. One of the first places we visited was Korah, a small town where the original community had been a leper colony. Today, it is a town steeped in deep poverty, where people live in makeshift huts and do anything they can just to stay alive. Great Hope Ministries sponsors an orphanage within the community. Along with the children they feed, they also serve meals to older men who suffer the effects of leprosy, including the loss of all their fingers. One day another team member, Andrew Bache, and I had the opportunity to feed some of these men. Layers of emotion swept over me, and my heart was completely overwhelmed and humbled by the profoundness of what we were doing. *I'm feeding a leper.* It was a moment—just like washing those kids' feet—in which Visiting Orphans had opened the door for me to do something that mattered more than anything else I'd ever done in my life.

The first day I was to lead worship for the kids, I thought I'd have about an hour with them, only to be told I had to fill three hours. I found out quickly that the kids there are encouraged not to dance. This was completely contrary to the experience I had in Uganda, and I wondered how this was going to work out over the next few days. Thankfully, a few here and there began to relax and started singing and dancing. Before the session was over, we were all having a pretty good time.

We went to visit women who were referred to as the "bead ladies" the next morning. In a shed-like barn with little light and no windows, these women made bracelets and necklaces all day long to sell for food. But before they began their arduous task, they shared a special prayer time early in the morning. The passion with which they worshipped was inspiring. I'd seen one day in the life of these people, and all that they had to do to survive. So, I couldn't blame them if they felt there was no reason to believe there was anything worth believing in. Unlike those of us living in the richest country in the world, their circumstances didn't deter them from expressing their joy.

Later, as I was pondering that morning's experience, I thought about how many people back home wouldn't even open their mouths or take their hands out of their pockets during worship. I felt the Lord saying, *There are those who have nothing, yet have everything . . . and those who have everything, yet have nothing.*

ON OUR LAST DAY IN ADDIS ABABA WE WENT TO MINISTER TO A community of people who live in the city dump. Literally. It was pretty miraculous that we could go in; most of the time the guards posted at the dump wouldn't permit outsiders to go in because it is so horrific.

It had been raining throughout the night, and when we began our slow walk up the rising heap of trash, my tennis shoes were squishing and sinking down into the muck and mire of the putrid refuse. The smell of the place was awful, and the air was full of swarms of flies.

When we got up high enough to the community, I saw dogs attacking the weakest member of their pack. I thought to myself, *I'm walking into Hell.* The families lived in makeshift tents, and they collected food and clothing after dump trucks dropped their loads. I was standing with a man named David who lived there. As we were talking, he pointed to a truck and said, "That one is from Ethiopian Airlines." Because the community members knew there was usually a lot of food wasted on those aircrafts, they were eager to get as close as they could to the wave of waste that dropped from the truck's cargo. They stood directly under the debris as it fell from the truck because it was easier to catch it that way. Their greatest hope was to catch a few intact utensil packets, complete with plastic knives, forks, and spoons and, even better, packets of sugar, salt, and pepper. You'd have thought they were catching gold by the way they poured those sugar packets into their mouths.

As I watched this scene of desperation, I realized that just a few days prior I had been a passenger on an Ethiopian Airlines jet, and that some of the food pouring out of that truck might have been my own.

I've been fortunate to have traveled to some of the most beautiful places in the world, including Waimea Canyon along the Napoli Coast on the Hawaiian island of Kauia, which is what I imagine the Garden of Eden might have looked like.

But that day in Ethiopia, I felt like I was in the worst place I had ever been. I don't know that I'll ever see anything as tragic. Life doesn't get any lower than living in a dump. What made it even worse was that there was no name for this community because the government didn't want the rest of the world to know people live there.

How do you process such a contrast between two places? I thought I had seen the "least of these" in other locales I'd visited . . . but none of them compared to this. When we got back on the van to return to the guest house at the orphanage twenty minutes away, we rode in complete silence.

Only a day later, I boarded an Ethiopian Air jet for the twenty-one-hour flight back to the United States. Just a few hours into the flight, the attendant set a tray of food in front of me. My mind immediately went back to that garbage dump in Addis Ababa and the vision of those people laying in wait under a dump truck. It was more than I could handle. Tears immediately filled my eyes, and I refused to eat the food. I felt a connection to those people because I now knew what they had to do to survive and hoped that my sealed tray of food would provide one of them with something good to eat.

I remembered people calling me an Isaiah 61 man because in that scripture Isaiah tells the oppressed that God "has sent me to comfort the broken-hearted" and that captives would be set free. I thought about the words to "One More Broken Heart" that I wrote for Point of Grace and the young prisoners at the Spencer Youth Center who inspired that song.

The Lord has taught me a lot about perspective. My heart was aching for all the orphans in Africa and the community of people living on a garbage dump. I wondered how anything could be done to fix such massive problems. *Just a little at a time*, He reassured me. *I sent you there this past week; you released My love and you made a difference.*

I'm grateful to know that many positive steps are being taken by people around the world, who have a passionate desire to bring deliverance in these situations. I am reminded of the Apostle Paul's words in Ephesians 6:15: *Your desire to tell the good news about peace should be like shoes on your feet.*

I thought about those yellow and red shoes sitting in my closet. I couldn't wait to get home, lace them back up, and see where the Lord would lead next.

CHAPTER 22

BLIND TRUST

I will sing to the Lord as long as I live.
I will praise my God to my last breath.

—Psalm 104:33

I WENT TO NEW YORK CITY FOR A FEW DAYS IN OCTOBER 2012 TO MEET with Derek Britt, a gifted television and film producer, and talk to him about the direction of this book. Derek believed in this project from day one, and, even though his schedule was filled to the max, he wanted to help us find a publisher. Until this day, we had spent almost a year talking to publishing companies that might be interested in my story. Skyhorse Publishing had offered a contract at the very beginning of the project in December 2011.

While we sat down for lunch at The Breslin in Manhattan and discussed the fact that Skyhorse Publishing had "been there" from the beginning, I was feeling more strongly than ever that no matter what other options came into the mix, Skyhorse was where God seemed to be leading us. And like so many times in my life—as you have seen throughout this book—His desire became very clear on that beautiful fall day in the city.

It was Wednesday, October 17, and two things happened that left no doubt about the direction of this project. First, that morning when I checked my emails, I saw an email blast from the Brentwood Benson Music marketing department that *The Christmas Shoe Tree* had become the number-one-selling kids' Christmas musical of the year. That was a pretty good way to start the day. Then, while we were having lunch, Derek received a text from Skyhorse Publishing announcing that its author, Mo Yan, had been awarded the Nobel Prize in Literature. That's an amazing feat for a company that has only been around since 2006. In that short time, though, it has proven its ability to publish great books, as evidenced by its four *New York Times'* best-sellers. That sealed the deal as far as I was concerned, because there was no doubt God was opening this door.

Remember my affinity for numbers? Well, seventeen was the prominent number of the day. It was October 17, and my "Jeff Slaughter VBS World Tour" for 2013, which was written after I finished *The Christmas Shoe Tree*, marked the seventeenth Vacation Bible School I have written. Seventeen is the number of victory. My heart was overwhelmed by how God had brought victory into my life and so richly blessed my first project with Brentwood Benson, a company who believed in me and had taken a giant leap of faith with me.

A FEW WEEKS LATER ON A COLD, DREARY DECEMBER SUNDAY MORNING, I found myself wrestling with whether I should stay home to attend "Bedside Baptist" or actually go to my home church, Grace Center. My mind was going through the pros and cons for both. I was tired from a hectic travel schedule, and that day would have been my niece Mallorie's twenty-ninth birthday. As you can imagine, her birthday is always very bittersweet. I was definitely leaning toward a laid-back morning sitting on the couch and drinking a big cup of coffee. But I kept feeling the Lord nudging me to get up and go to church. I relented, got dressed, and hopped in the car.

When I walked into Grace Center near Brentwood, Tennessee, I had no idea that R.T. Kendall, a retired preacher who was the guest speaker that morning, would rock my world the way he did over the next hour. Had I not dragged myself from my house to hear his message, I'd have missed out on yet another incredible gift the Lord wanted to give me.

As Mr. Kendall began to teach that day, he invited the congregation to "turn to Habakkuk, chapter two," and my eyes widened. "We'll start with verse two." My verse! My heart raced as I remembered reading that scripture for the first time when I was nine years old. Then my thoughts immediately turned to the moment I was standing before the glass case that contained the Dead Seas Scrolls in Jerusalem.

As Mr. Kendall preached his message that morning, I began to feel an even deeper connection to Habakkuk than I ever had. This prophet had experienced great pain and was troubled by what he had witnessed. He saw a dying world, and it broke his heart. So he sought answers to some very difficult questions. He wondered about the evil all around and why those who were wicked always seemed to win.

"Habakkuk is basically asking God, 'Why did you create us when you knew all these bad things were going to happen?'" Mr. Kendall offered. He expounded on how God had told Habakkuk that he may not get the answers he was looking for until the "end times" which, in effect, meant he might not know until he saw the Lord face to face. Habakkuk had to accept that. "Think about Abraham and Moses, two of the greatest men in the Old Testament," Mr. Kendall pointed out. "They suffered through many difficulties in their own lives; however, in choosing to keep their hope and trust in the Lord, they had a profound impact on humanity. The greater the anointing, the greater the suffering you'll have to go through."

I don't know how many people were in the building that morning, but it was as if R.T. Kendall was talking only to me. When he revealed that Habakkuk's acceptance of God's answer came when he had chosen to "forgive God" through his disappointments and trials, I thought about my mama, and how long it had taken me to forgive God after she died.

Ultimately, Habakkuk's greatest triumph came with the realization that no matter what happens, God continuously demonstrates both His power and His love, and hands them out in equal measure: "Even though the fig trees have no blossoms, and there are no grapes on the vines; even though the olive crop fails, and the fields lie empty and barren; even though the flocks die in the fields, and the cattle barns are empty, yet I will rejoice in the Lord! I will be joyful in the God of my salvation! The Sovereign Lord is my strength! He makes me as surefooted as a deer, able to tread upon the heights" (Habakkuk 3:17–19).

Sometimes we want answers to life's circumstances right now, as if we are entitled to an explanation. There have been many "right now" moments for me, and I've had to wait—sometimes for long periods of time—to get any answers. I identify with Habakkuk in that respect. But if we make a choice to bless others without condition, God will increase our anointing. Over the past couple of years, the Lord has been teaching me a lot about praying blessings over the people, situations, and companies involved in my life. No matter what. He tells us to bless unconditionally. And God has returned those blessings upon me. I have felt a greater anointing in many areas of my life, particularly in leading worship. I have come to discover that when He doesn't answer our prayers as quickly or as specifically as we would like, it's only because He has something better in store for us.

I have certainly found it to be true through times of pain and loss as much as through laughter and joy, through uncomfortable life transitions and death, to coming through shameful sexual abuse. Looking back, I haven't enjoyed any of those hardships—who does?—and there are many things I've experienced that I would not wish on anyone. But I know, without a doubt, that it was all part of the purpose God had assigned to me even before He created the heavens and the earth.

There is clear evidence of God's sovereign work in our lives and how He orchestrates events that bless our faith and trust and ultimately honor Him. I believe God sent me to New York City for that three-day period in 2012 to show both me and Derek how two people who barely knew each other could accomplish something together that could only be explained by Him. This book has been ordained by God in the hopes that whoever reads it will find encouragement to press on. Nothing in it about me means anything. Everything in it about Him does.

Most of the books we read have a clear beginning and a clear ending. The body of the story is sandwiched in between, and once we finish that last word on that last page, the story is usually resolved. But that's not the case with me. This is not the end of my story. For as long as I am breathing and moving and living, God will continue to work His story through me.

And the same is true for you.

Do you remember Stephen, the blind kid at camp? He jumped. Boy, did he jump! He ran with reckless abandon, and when his daddy told him to jump, he flung his body as far through the air as he could. As the momentum of his body hit that gigantic gray tarp all slippery with soap and water, he glided all the way to the end, and rolled out onto the sticky, wet grass on the other side. His laughter could be heard throughout the recreation field.

You see, in trusting his father, he experienced victory. Even in total darkness, he never hesitated to jump when his daddy told him to, because he never considered that his daddy might leave him, or try to hurt him. He had learned that if he listened, obeyed, and completely trusted his dad—it didn't matter how dark the circumstances—there was laughter and joy on the other side.

My Heavenly Father has proven that He can be trusted as well. And when He told me to trust Him and "jump" into the new opportunities He had waiting for me, I wanted to be like my buddy Stephen. While there was more than a little trepidation, I believed that if I obeyed with blind trust—even if I couldn't see what was on the other side—laughter and joy would be there for me as well.

If I have learned anything in my life, if there is something I have no doubt about, it is God's faithfulness and His desire to bless His children.

And in the end, I know God wins, Satan loses, and we will witness the greatest vindication that has ever been. I know this because God's Word says it. I have declared, and will continue to declare, all the days of my life that through every chapter, every verse, and every promise I have ever heard . . . it's all true.

AFTERWORD:
THE STORIES BEHIND THE SONGS

WE BELIEVE, FROM "RAMBLIN' ROAD TRIP" VBS, 2005

In the fall of 2003, I began working on the songs for LifeWay's "Ramblin' Road Trip" VBS, which was set to release in 2005. Daddy had passed away on March 19 of that year, and a week later I jumped back into a pretty heavy traveling schedule. All through the summer months, I was pretty much on auto-pilot emotionally. When I sat down to work on the "Roadtrip" songs in October, I felt completely empty and disconnected. The creative flow that I was used to having with the Lord seemed "stopped up." As I sat at the piano staring at a blank piece of paper, I felt the Lord say, *Go back to the basics . . . the basics of what you have believed about me all of your life.* I realized the things I had learned about the Lord as a child had built the foundation of what I was resting on now as I was learning how to live without my daddy. I felt impressed to write a song that would bring these foundational truths together. And if someone sang it and truly believed every word, that person's relationship with the Lord would be sealed without a doubt. All of sudden I heard myself playing the opening melody. Then the

Lord whispered the first line, *We believe and we are never the same.* Fifteen minutes later it was done. "We Believe" eventually became the first VBS song to "cross over" into the church as an anthem for adult choirs and was LifeWay's number-one-selling anthem that year!

SPEAK UP, FROM "ARCTIC EDGE" VBS, 2006

I've always loved including rap songs as much as possible in the musicals I write for kids. Though I am not a big fan of this style of music, I know most kids are, and I'm a firm believer that because God created music, you can redeem any style of music for His Kingdom! After the release of "Arctic Edge: Where Adventure Meets Courage" in 2006, I received an email from a children's choir director who had taught the VBS music class at her church. She told me about a twelve-year-old boy named Austin, who usually sat in the back row totally disengaged with what was going on in her class, until she played "Speak Up." All of a sudden he got into the song with everyone else. He was so excited, in fact, that he asked the director if he could get on the stage during the Worship Rally time and perform it with her! She was completely blown away by the transformation that took place in him. His parents actually came to see him help lead in the Worship Rally because they could not believe their shy, reserved son would get up to do something like this in front of so many people. By the end of the week, Austin had made a profession of faith to follow Christ.

My heart rejoiced until I read the next part of her letter. Three weeks after VBS, Austin was tragically killed when he was hit by a car while riding his bicycle. In an instant, my heart broke, and my mind raced back to that fateful day when Vickie and I stood over Mallorie and sang her into Heaven. The children's choir director told me how devastated Austin's family was and that because they didn't go to church, she didn't know them well, but the members of her church were reaching out to them as best they could.

I immediately called Vickie and asked her to write a letter to Austin's mom. She wrote a stunning letter that only one who has walked that road could . . . from one mother's broken heart to another. She ended it by sharing Psalm 126:5 with her: "Those who sow in tears shall reap with joyful shouting." She explained how they both had planted "seeds" (their children) in the ground with tears and great agony, but the Lord promised that somehow there would be a harvest of joy!

After Austin's mom received Vickie's letter, she wrote her right back, thanking her and telling her that the harvest had already begun! A week after the accident, Austin's parents did go to church, and at the end of the service, his father walked the aisle and accepted the Lord! He told the pastor how Austin had come home from VBS singing some rap song about speaking up and couldn't wait to go back the next day. A couple days later he told his parents all about his decision to follow Jesus. After Austin passed, his father, instead of getting angry and completely shutting the door on the Lord, did the exact opposite. He knew his son had gone to heaven, and he was determined to meet him there. He began to pray and seek the Lord for comfort and walked that aisle the week after his son's death. How could he have ever known that God would use his own son to lead him to salvation? Sound kind of familiar? Truly the harvest had begun, and I praise God for allowing me the honor of writing something that touched the heart of a twelve-year-old boy whose final act on this earth was to lead his daddy to the Lord.

I Will, from "Big Apple Adventure" VBS, 2011

I shared a great deal about this particular VBS in the book, but there's still one more story I have to tell you. I've tried throughout my ministry to write certain songs to help kids memorize scriptures and other facts from the Bible I think are important for them to know. In 2001 I wrote a song for "Truth Trackers and the Secret of the Stone Tablets" that taught kids the Ten Commandments. In 2002 I wrote one that taught about the specific things the Lord made on each day of creation. When I began writing for "Big Apple" and realized the Day Four scripture verse was the "Great Commission" passage, I knew I wanted the chorus of the song to flow as closely to those verses as I could make it. As I was working through the song, I heard the Lord whisper to me to use a section of the old hymn "Take the Name of Jesus with You" for the bridge. The chorus of that hymn goes,

> *Precious Name, oh how sweet*
> *Hope of earth and joy of Heav'n*
> *Precious Name, oh how sweet*
> *Hope of earth and joy of Heav'n*

I thought it was a perfect compliment to the song and being able to teach kids another great hymn of our faith was an added bonus!

Once we began promoting "Big Apple" at the VBS Institutes and Previews LifeWay hosts around the country, a lady came up to me and told me how excited she was about this song. "Did you know that Lydia Baxter, the woman who wrote the hymn 'Take the Name of Jesus With You,' was a missionary in New York City?" Obviously the setting for "Big

Apple" was New York City, and immediately I knew that I needed to find out more about Lydia Baxter. I had a feeling the Lord was about to show me something "bigger than the apple"!

As I read though her biography, I found that she was born in New York, that she was a missionary in New York City and surrounding areas, and that she and her sister planted a church in an area of the city where one had never been before! How many women were doing that in the 1800s? Then I noticed her birthday and froze. It was September 2, 1809. Lynne Norris had called me with the 2011 VBS theme on September 2, 2009. I could feel the Lord telling me, *I never forget my own, or the things they have done for Me. Lydia is my special girl who had a deep passion for New York City and laid her life down to serve there. So, I made a way for her to be remembered and honored in this VBS, and, yes, it was created on her birthday.*

My legs felt weak. I remember thinking, *Lord, every day You teach more about the depth of Your love for us.* Whenever I share this story with kids, I tell them, "That's how He loves us you guys! He is our Daddy who rejoices and sings over us and is so proud of things we do for Him. And He never forgets!"

BECAUSE, FROM "BOOMERANG EXPRESS" VBS, 2009

"Boomerang Express" was unusual in that it actually took place in two locations. The storyline of the daily drama was based around a skyping session between two boys in Australia and a girl in Israel. Each day the Bible study was an excerpt from the story of the relationship between Jesus and Peter. I've shared with you the tremendous things the Lord did while I was in Israel, but it wasn't until the summer of 2009 was almost over that He revealed an even greater work He had done through this program.

I was in the middle of my Centri-Kid camps at Ridgecrest, North Carolina, when I stopped in the lobby of the reception area to check my email. I had received one from a children's pastor in Alabama, who told me about a boy named Ethan. He was shy, but was faithfully coming each day to VBS. Wednesday of that week was the day the music class was to learn "Because," the video for which I had filmed in front of the Garden Tomb. The pastor said she felt the Lord telling her to try a different approach when she introduced this song to the kids. And so, she asked them to bow their heads and just listen to the recording. She challenged them to really sense the Lord speaking to them.

When it was over, she asked if anyone had anything to share. Ethan raised his hand and said that he felt the Lord tell him it was time for them to become friends. So she stopped and explained to the whole class how to begin a relationship with Christ and become "friends" with Him. After the class she prayed with Ethan, and he accepted the Lord as his Savior.

On the way home from VBS that afternoon, Ethan was killed in a car accident. And once again I called Vickie to write a note to Ethan's mother. As I walked back to the auditorium to begin the evening worship service, my heart was so heavy and sad, yet I was also rejoicing because I knew where Ethan was. He had probably already met Mallorie, and I imagined her showing him around. I also had this burning desire to make Ethan's short life matter. When I walked on the stage, I told the kids what had happened, and I asked them all to pray with me for Ethan's family. You could hear a pin drop at first, but then the sweet sound of their voices murmuring around the room, lifting their innocent prayers to the Father, was euphoric.

The next night we were collecting a love offering that would go to help various missionaries around the world. Each church was given a special bag to use to collect money from members of its group. One kid from each group was chosen to bring the bag down front and place it in one of the baskets on stage. As we went through the baskets later that night, we noticed that almost all the churches had placed two bags in the basket instead of one. Each extra bag was marked something like, "For Ethan's family," or "In memory of Ethan." When I walked back outside to hang out with the kids before bedtime, pastors left and right told me that the kids in their groups had come up with the idea of the extra offering for Ethan, not the adults.

I've always believed that kids are way more sophisticated than we give them credit for and that they can go deeper in worship than anyone would ever expect. I know this because I've witnessed it for almost thirty years. One of my favorite verses has always been I Timothy 4:12: "Don't let anyone look down on you because you're young." It's through situations like these when that truth is reinforced in my heart even stronger. What a beautiful thing to see children display the heart of the Father and realize that they're not too young to be the body of Christ to a family in need.

THE WORD, FROM "OUTRIGGER ISLAND," 2008

I've always loved creating musical tapestries that blend scriptures with melodies that actually sound like what the words are saying. It's a great tool to help people memorize God's word quickly and to "hide it in their hearts." I realized years ago when I was writing the song "It's All True" that there are not a lot of songs that actually talk *about* and honor God's Word as a whole. That's why I've always loved that song so much.

When I sat down to work on "Outrigger Island" in the fall of 2006, I saw an opportunity to write another song like that. Day Four was usually the day I chose for the ballad, or "the pretty song" as my dear friend Lynne Norris always referred to it. I began to hear the opening melody, and the first words came quickly: "In the beginning was the Word." I could feel a heavy anointing in the room. I knew I needed to look up the reference in order to finish this verse, but I couldn't remember where it was. I thought it might be John, but wasn't sure. I didn't want to break the momentum, so I thought, *Lord, You can tell me where this verse is. Help me find it.* Instantly I heard the familiar whisper in my spirit, *John 1:1.* I flipped to the Gospel of John, and my eyes fell upon Chapter 1, Verse 1: "In the beginning was the Word; the Word was with God and was God." As I continued writing the song, I could feel that the Lord was pouring music and lyrics into my heart that were straight from His Throne Room . . . from the Secret Place.

When we went to record this song with the kids, I felt compelled to tell them something I never had in years past. I said, "You guys, let's ask angels to sing along with us on these tracks and add a sound from Heaven on them! And that when people listen to this song, they will know there's something different about it, and they will be overwhelmed by the power and anointing of the Holy Spirit." Well, we prayed, and we asked. The kids sang it in one take, and you could definitely hear something different—an extra "layer"—in their sound. I always pray for our recording sessions to be more like worship times, and this one definitely was!

A few months later, our video crew, Bill and Tim Cox, Rick Sims, Steve Fralick, Lynne Norris, and I traveled to the island of Kauai to film the choreography videos on different beaches around the island. We were trying to capture the "golden hour" of late afternoon sunlight as the backdrop for "The Word." I was standing at the water's edge facing the crew so that they were facing the water and the sunset. Well, the Lord started "showin' out" (as Mama would have put it)! You wouldn't believe the way the clouds and beams of light were shifting and reflecting off the water. Finally, Bill said, "Let's shoot a 'real' music video. We have to do something special with this kind of beauty." So we shot about ten more takes at different angles, trying to capture the incredible sky.

As we were filming the last take, it started to rain.

I thought, *Oh, no, Lord! This is the best take we've done, and my shirt and my hair are going to get wet and ruin it.* Then I heard Him say, *Don't worry, this is Me.* I began to notice that neither my shirt nor my hair was getting wet. Bill, who was behind the camera, pulled away and looked directly at me. There was confusion in his face. I saw the others get up and look at the monitor and then at me. As soon as we were finished, Bill told me that the rain didn't show up on the camera. We could all feel it and see it, but it wasn't registering on the screen. Before I could say anything, Lynne said, "You know, I could feel the Lord telling me that this was the rain of the Holy Spirit falling on us . . . and that's a different kind of rain."

ACKNOWLEDGMENTS

From Jeff: Thank you, Randy Winton for pushing . . . and pushing . . . and pushing me to do this. Ha ha! Hey, it only took two years, right? You wouldn't give up and helped me turn a dream into reality. Derek, Holly, and Courtney, y'all rock the Casbah! Thanks for your support, patience, and belief in this book! Amy, Michael, Tom, and Kim, I am honored that this book is wrapped with your blessings! Vickie and Carla, my nephews, nieces, "aun-tees" and uncles, and all the cousins, I'm so grateful for the memories we've made and will continue to make together. Reed and Sammie Smith, thank you for being my adopted Tennessee parents. I love you dearly! Randy Cox, thanks for opening the first door. Sandra Parker, you were the "catalyst." The Lord used you to show me what He made me for when you asked me to lead worship for my first kids' camp twenty-seven years ago. Throughout the years, I have continually been amazed by the incredible guys the Lord has brought alongside me to be a part of my band! Thank you, Jonathon, Wesley, and Todd Durbin; Brandon Turner, Chris Jackson, brothers Phil and Mark Snowden, Dan Runnels, Brad McKelvey, Justin Burns, Jeremy McCullough, Mark Owens, and Jordan Vincent. What a joy it's been to make music in the "worship room" with you! All of you have given me more than I could ever repay! Thank you for demonstrating your love for the Lord in the way you have loved me and the kids we have led in worship. Preston and Spencer Dalton, the Lord knows exactly who to bring into our lives at just the right time. Mark, Andrea, "Patti" (Amy F.), Carl, Leann, Linda, Levi, Suzanne, Luke, Christa, Kurt, Ellen, Lynne, "G-Love," Nathan, Dena, "Domino," Andrew, Matt, and "Mommy Rita". . . LOVE, LOVE, LOVE YOU ALL! Michael D. (BF), I finally did it!

From Randy: I want to thank Jeff Slaughter for the privilege of writing his story . . . finally. After two years of convincing him to share a story that would encourage all who read it, he finally relented. Over the past fifteen months, there has been much laughter, many tears, and a book that we can be proud of . . . a book I know God is going to bless and use for His glory. To my parents, David and Marie Winton, who I've come to appreciate more and more every day. To my "favorite" in-laws, David and Linda Kell, who accepted me as their son the minute I fell in love with their daughter and have always been so encouraging. To my sister, Tammy Summey, who always sees the good in everybody, and my "little" brother, Brian Winton, who I've always looked up to. To all the students in my ministry over the last eighteen years who have both challenged and inspired me, and especially those at FBC Brewton in Alabama. They sang Jeff's songs with such passion as children and have grown up to teach me what it truly means to minister to each other. You have loved and embraced my family and I'm humbled to have been able to walk side-by-side with you these eleven years as your youth minister on this faith journey. To Dr. Tommy and Martha Smith, who have mentored my sons and encouraged me as a youth minister, father, husband, and author. It is at that cozy cabin on their farm where the majority of this book was written and where all of the interviews with Jeff took place. Thank you for honoring both of us on this endeavor. Every author needs a friend who will read and offer critical advice on how chapters affect them. So, thank you to my lifelong friend, Lesli Boyd, who read all the bits and pieces of this book over the last six months. Your suggestions and encouraging words were invaluable. To our new friend, Holly Rubino (aka "Grammar Girl"), who somehow made it through nearly a year as our editor. In God's wisdom, He prompted Skyhorse Publishing to assign its very best—a brilliant Connecticut girl—to read and correct every story a Mississippi boy (Jeff) was telling and a Tennessee boy (Randy) was writing. One day we'll all have to sit down at a big table and eat a bowl of cheese grits. To Derek Britt, who believed in this book from the very beginning and whose efforts led to Skyhorse Publishing believing in it as well. I am forever grateful to both for the opportunity. To Jack Fitts, Chase Clower, Todd Ray, Edna Knowles and Tammy Stanford . . . I can't think of a better "team" to work with side-by-side in ministry at FBC Brewton.